P9-DUU-056

AUSTRALIA

AUSTRALIA

PHOTOGRAPHY BY ERNST WRBA TEXT BY KLAUS VIEDEBANTT

KONECKY & KONECKY

Konecky & Konecky
150 Fifth Ave.
New York, NY

Translation by Sibylle Dausien and Sean Konecky

Copyright © Econ Ullstein List Verlag
GmbH & Co. KG, Munchen. Published 1990,
1998 by Sudwest Verlag

Translation Copyright © 2000 by
W.S. Konecky Associates, Inc.

All rights reserved

ISBN: 1-56852-277-0

Printed in Italy

*A journey in pictures through Australia: a house on
Kangaroo Island; the Whitsunday Archipelago;
eucalyptus trees in Kakadu National Park; a gaily
coloured parrot; eucalyptus trees in the outback.*

PRECEDING SPREAD:
The Pinnacles in Western Australia.

PRECEDING SPREAD:

Melbourne is the capital of the State of Victoria and the second largest city in the country after Sydney. In the attractive inner city with its broad avenues lined with trees, a relaxed atmosphere prevails, enhanced by the many parks of which its inhabitants are justly proud. Most of the city's places of interest are easy to reach on foot, but it's also worth taking the tram down to the Yarra river.

The State of Queensland lies in northeastern Australia. As one travels north, the land becomes less densely populated. Around Brisbane can be found the Gold Coast and the Sunshine Coast, the latter a favourite spot for vacationers. Further up, the coast becomes even more peaceful until the traveller reaches the exquisite Great Barrier Reef. In the northernmost part of the state, on Cape York, there is nothing but unspoiled tropical forest.

The MacDonnell Ranges in the heart of Australia's outback holds precious water holes within its ravines. Accordingly, vegetation here is richer than in the rest of the outback. Eucalyptus trees abound. In the surrounding countryside parching heat prevails year round. One should not attempt to travel through this area without careful preparations to guarantee the supply of water.

Entirely different is the climate of the land surrounding Darwin in the Northern Territory. This tropical region has no lack of water, especially during rainy season. In monsoon season, from November to April, it can bear the brunt of violent cyclones that come down from the Timor Sea. Flooding is common. The Fog Dam Conservation Preserve to the east of Darwin is particularly rich in bird life.

The Sixth Continent

In the beginning there was Baiame, the Spirit Father, the creator of the world. Baiame looked at his work but was dissatisfied. Something was missing. There was one creature full of spirit still to be created, one that could recognise its master. Baiame journeyed down from heaven.

Yhi, the Sun, disappeared and it got dark; nervous animals sought refuge in a cave. Every now and then, one of them would go to the entrance of the cave to see if the light had returned. When it was Goanna the Serpent's turn, he came back and told them about a new kind of light, like a moon, but very close to the ground. The hawk, not believing him, flew out of the cave and returned with the report that it was a kangaroo. "But there is something very strange about this kangaroo. He has eyes like stars," he said. Now all the animals streamed to the entrance of the cave and each returned with a different version of what he had seen. And so there was discord among the animals.

Baiame was troubled; even though all the animals were his created spirits, none of them knew him for what he was. The Father of the World decided to shape a being that would recognise its creator, and therefore created Man. Yhi looked upon this new creation and was pleased. So the Sun returned to the world and all the creatures came out of the cave. And Man was aware of all that took place around him.

Kangaroo Island lies offshore from the city of Adelaide. The south coast on the open ocean is, like that of Victoria, wild and rugged and pounded by the surf.

For thousands of years this story of creation has been passed down through the generations, but different tribes tell it with some variation. Some call the Great Father, 'Bunjil', some 'Nooralie', and some have other names. But the belief in a supernatural creative power is common to all aboriginal peoples.

Though the story of creation recounts the origins of man and the other animals native to Australia, little mention is made of the origins of the earth itself. Scientists today are still uncertain as to how the earth arrived at its present state of formation. But they do have a much better idea of how the sixth continent came into existence. Originally, it was a part of Gondwana, one of the two ur-continents from which the earth as we know it today has come into being. About two hundred million years ago, the original landmass of the planet split into two at the equator. Gondwana, named after a region in India, formed the Southern hemisphere. This great continent further split into what are present-day Africa, South America, India, Antarctica and Australia.

For long after, the land 'Australia', as it was later named, was empty of people. From the perspective of geological time, its inhabitation took place at a fairly recent date. About 40,000 years ago, during the last global ice age, there was so much ice around the two poles that the sea level around Australia was 180 metres lower than it is today. As a result, the island of New Guinea was connected to Australia, and at the same time, much of Indonesia belonged to the Asian continent. The islands between the two great landmasses made it possible to cross to the Australian continent on simple boats. That is how the aboriginal peoples settled Australia; there they remained, cut off by the rising sea level as the earth began to warm again, in

The coastal region of northern Queensland is an endless ribbon of sandy beach.

however, Tasman did not realise that he had discovered an island. Similarly, when he set foot on New Zealand some time later, he did not notice that there was a second adjacent island.

After Tasman's return, it was still an open question as to where the great southern continent lay. (The scientists of the day thought that such a land mass was necessary for the earth to be balanced.) There were many who speculated, upon learning of Tasman's discovery of New Zealand, that he had found the west coast of this southern continent. The search for Australia was still continuing in 1768, when Captain James Cook set off from England on his first trip to the Pacific. His official charge was to engage in astronomical observations from the recently discovered island of Tahiti. But he also had orders that he should proceed west from Tahiti in search of the mysterious southern continent.

In October of 1769, he reached Tasman's New Zealand, where he soon recognised that these were islands and not part of a larger continent. He set off once again, striking a westerly course towards Van Diemens Land. Strong winds drove his small craft north, which resulted in unexpected consequences. On April 20, the word was "Land Ahoy!" as the *Endeavour* arrived on the southeast coast of Australia. Cook noted in his logbook: "The weather which being clear gave us an opportunity to View the Country, which had a very agreeable and promising aspect, diversified with hills, ridges, plains and Valleys, with some few small lawns: but for the most part the whole slope was covered with wood, the hills and ridges rise with a gentle slope;

stone-age isolation for many thousands of years.

The first European visitors were Dutch. They came from their colony in Indonesia to explore the north and west coasts of Australia, and called the land New Holland. But they were disappointed by what they found there — the land was barren, and promised none of the riches that were discovered on Borneo and Java. It was mainly a hot desert with no sign of gold, so interest in this 'economic wasteland' quickly evaporated. The Dutch mapped the coastal regions but had no idea of the vast extent of land beyond. In 1642, Abel Janszoon Tasman discovered an island that he named Van Diemens Land (today, it bears his name and is known as Tasmania). Not being a very good observer,

they are not high, neither are there many of them." On April 28, Cook, who had sailed north following the coastline, found a bay where he could weigh anchor. Joseph Banks and Daniel Solander, two scientists travelling with the expedition, found the land filled with numerous hitherto unknown varieties of plants. This inspired Cook to name his discovery Botany Bay.

The 'First Fleet' Sets Out

Cook and his men made landfall in the spring. The countryside looked rich and green. Accordingly, the reports from Cook and the impressionable Banks were very positive. His majesty King George III's advisors saw this newly discovered land as an immediate solution to a pressing problem. Harsh laws and constant fears of civil unrest had created an explosion in England's prison population, and war in the American colonies had not only deprived the crown of one of its most valuable possessions, but also stopped the export of convicts. Australia was seen as the ideal alternative. On May 13 1787, the First Fleet, composed of eleven ships, started its journey to establish the first European settlement in Australia. At the beginning of the following year, the fleet reached its destination.

Once there, the prison colony was founded — not a glorious beginning to a new chapter in world history. The 750 prisoners included 190 women and 13 children, not all of whom were criminals. Some, mostly Irish, had been transported for political reasons, but all of them were

driven by hunger. Obviously, they were not what one would call 'perfectly qualified' to make the new settlement a success. The same was true for the guards. However, the fleet commander and subsequently first governor of the new colony of "New South Wales " (NSW), Captain Arthur Phillip, was a conscientious man. This officer, who was of German descent, (his father was a teacher in Frankfurt) recognized immediately that Botany Bay was not a promising site for a settlement, despite the glowing reports of Cook and Banks. In January, at the height of the summer, the bay was dry, and there was a lack of fresh water. Phillip decided to explore further and discovered what turned out to be one of the most beautiful places on earth, now known as the Bay of Sydney. Cook, in fact, had

The tropical coast near Cairns. Although delightfully situated, this area is mainly used as a jumping off point for tourists en route to the Great Barrier Reef.

Only after the creation of the man-made Lake Argyll in Western Australia, which guaranteed a secure water supply, was it possible for this area to become populated.

passed by the bay and even gave it a name, Port Jackson.

On January 26 1788, Governor Phillip raised the British flag over the bay. That date is now celebrated as Australia Day, a national holiday. But for the first white settlers of the new continent there was little cause to celebrate. To the contrary, the nascent colony was destined to endure many hard years, during which the scarcity of food exacerbated the harsh conditions of prison life.

Rum in exchange for money

The chronic shortage of food was not the only problem the new governour had to face. His soldiers and his prisoners got into bloody fights with the aboriginal population. Phillip's government was torn with many internal conflicts, but somehow he managed to keep things under control until the first free settlers found their way to the new continent.

After leading the colony for four years, Phillips resigned his post. His successor, Francis Grose, was unable to rein in his soldiers. The military, corrupted by the lack of hindrances to its free exercise of power, was soon running the economy. Rum became the regular medium of exchange. They became known as the " Rum Corps" a bitter name in Australian history. One of their civilian assistants, a shady businessman named John Macarthur, unwittingly laid the foundation for Australia's later wealth: he introduced sheep farming.

Macarthur's intrigues and the corrupted morals of the military would lead to the downfall of the colony's next governor, Captain William Bligh. The former commander of the legendary *HMS Bounty* who, in 1789, survived the most famous mutiny in the annals of naval history, sailed a small open boot with those of his men who remained loyal to him, from Tonga to Timor. He became governor of New South Wales in 1805. There he survived two rebellions. At one point, he was taken prisoner by his own men. They did not approve of his efforts to bring an end to the Rum Corps.

Sydney's first blossom

In 1810, when Lachlan Macquarie became governor, things changed. He brought his own troops to Australia and managed to overturn the corrupt Rum Corps. In so doing, he brought peace and order to the Colony. Under his guidance, Sydney began to blossom. In 1813, Gregory Blaxland, William Lawson and William Wentworth succeeded in crossing the Blue Mountains, lying to the west of the city. On the other side, they discovered fertile land waiting to be developed that would provide badly needed food for the colony.

Melbourne was officially founded in 1823. Thanks to its gold mines it would, in time, rival Sydney. As early as 1823, gold strikes had been reported, but with a major discovery at Summerhill Creek in New South Wales, the gold rush began. People swarmed north from Melbourne. To slow down the exodus, the newly-founded colony of Victoria declared a market price for gold. Shortly after this initial success, richly productive mining operations were undertaken in Ballarat. These developments transformed Melbourne into the financial capital of Australia, and it has remained such up to the present day in contrast to Sydney, which has always been regarded as the cultural center of the country.

But we are getting a bit ahead of ourselves. The discovery of gold brought in its train a rapid surge in population. By 1860, 650,000 people had streamed into Australia lured by the promise of gold, more than doubling the original population of 400,000, But it did not stop there. New gold strikes in Queensland (1867) and then in Western Australia led to further migrations, and this number increased after more gold mines were found in these regions. In

1880, there were over two million inhabitants of European descent; by 1905, more than four million (in 1992, the population of Australia was 17.8 million). The necessity of feeding and housing this great influx of people fuelled an economic boom.

These developments had both negative and positive social consequences. The white gold miners envied their hard-working Chinese competitors and the continual hostilities between them led, in later years, to the establishment of a 'White Australian Policy'. Though never officially admitted, the effect of this policy was to make only white emigrants feel welcome. It was not until the 1970s that this de facto apartheid policy changed.

One of the most appealing features of Sydney is its location on the ocean. It is hard to believe that such ideal conditions for all kinds of water sports are so close to a major metropolis.

On the Barricades

The positive social developments that stemmed from the great gold discoveries were punctuated by one violently suppressed rebellion: in 1854, gold miners in Ballarat protested against what they thought were extreme assaying fees. The revolt quickly spread. General discontent over the usurpation of the people's rights by their government led the protesters out onto the barricades. They named their fortress Eureka Stockade after the tavern in which the movement had begun. Although the barricades were, eventually, stormed by the police, the rebellion signalled the beginning of a new democratic order.

Mapping out and then conquering the Australian continent required tremendous effort. By the 1840s, Australian explorers had fully navigated its coasts and major rivers. Special mention must be made of Matthew Flinders who, between 1801 and 1803, circumnavigated Australia and charted its coastline. Still, most of the land was in the interior, and this remained unknown territory. The first venture into the interior was the successful passage of the Blue Mountains, described above. In 1839, Edward John Eyre travelled inland from Adelaide. In the same year, the geologist Paul de Strzelecki scaled a 2,228-metre high mountain (the highest peak in the country) and named it, in honour of the Polish patriot, Mount Kosciusko. In 1844, Charles Sturt tried unsuccessfully to reach the north coast of the continent from Adelaide. In the same year, the German explorer, Ludwig Leichhardt, was more successful. He completed a trek

of over 4,800 kilometres from Brisbane to the north coast. In 1846, Leichhardt attempted to cross the continent from east to west, but he had to turn around after only 800 kilometres. In 1848, he set out once again, but his expedition was lost without a trace in the wasteland. The Australian novelist Patrick White, who won the Nobel Prize in 1973, based his book, *Voss*, on the adventures of this German explorer.

In 1862, John McDouall Stuart succeeded, on his third attempt, in crossing from Adelaide to the north coast. As a result of his successful journey, it became possible to lay a cable across the continent, and this facilitated rapid overseas communication with England.

The gas stations in the outback also serve as resting spots, where the traveller can replenish his supply of water and other necessities.

Capital in the Wilderness

Given the rivalry between Sydney and Melbourne, a new capital, Canberra, was chosen for the young state. It lay in a kind of 'no man's land' between the two great metropolitan centres. Walter Burley Griffin, a Chicago architect who had never been to the site, won the international competition for building the capital. He arrived in Australia in 1913 and immediately set out upon his still-celebrated endeavour. But it took another thirteen years for the move from the provisional capital of Melbourne to be completed.

In the meantime, great events were taking place in the outside world: a war that was to have ended all wars. Inevitably, Australia, as part of the British Commonwealth, became deeply involved. In the conflict, thousands of Australians lost their lives. Australia proved itself to be a valuable and loyal ally to Britain in this and subsequent wars.

To assist the British Armed Forces, Australia, together with New Zealand, formed a new Army, the Australian and New Zealand Army Corps (ANZAC). On April 25, 1915, the ANZAC troops were ordered to take Gallipoli, a peninsula in the Dardanelles, from the Germans and their allies, the Turks. For over six months, they tried in vain to oust the enemy from its entrenched position. By the end of the war, almost 7,700 Australian and New Zealand soldiers were accounted missing in action, and 33,532 had lost their lives. Since then, April 25 has been observed as ANZAC Day, in both Australia and New Zealand.

Outside of Darwin, horses are drawn to the cooling breezes of the sea.

Australia was on its way to becoming a recognised and established modern state. Gradually the sentiment developed, despite strong emotional ties to Great Britain, that Australia ought to assert itself as a fully independent nation. On the first of January 1901, independence was finally achieved. The new country comprised the states of New South Wales, Victoria, Tasmania, South Australia, Western Australia, Queensland and the Northern Territory, which was not granted full political rights. Some small islands were also made part of the newly formed nation.

At the Great Barrier Reef Wonderland in Townsville, one can observe the remarkable underwater world of the reef through thick glass.

Alliance with America

Though World War I ended in an Allied victory, it also resulted in the weakening of British might east of the Suez. Australians began to realise that their traditional partner in arms alone could not guarantee their security. They now found themselves turning more often to their American cousins. This was particularly the case in the years leading up to World War II, when the Japanese were expanding their sphere of influence. Nonetheless, with the onset of war in Europe, Australians once more rallied to England's defence. Australians were deployed in the Mediterranean to counter Nazi incursions, and a smaller contingent fought against the Japanese in Malaysia and Singapore. Their best efforts could

not, however, stop the onward march of the Japanese army, and the troops prepared themselves at Tenno against a threatened invasion. On February 19, 1942, Darwin was bombed. War had finally reached the shores of Australia. All hope rested on the Americans who, in the bloody battle of the Coral Sea, were able to halt the progress of the Japanese war machine. Australia did not forget their help and fought at their side during the Korean War. This was also the case in Vietnam, at least at the beginning. When, just as in the States, anti-war protests grew more vehement, Canberra withdrew a part of its forces.

The epoch after World War II witnessed greater changes in Australia than ever before. The reasons for this were not only the growing awareness of Great Britain's military weakness, but a natural maturation process by which the once-dependent nation grew apart from the Motherland. In addition, the ethnic composition of the population was distinctly altered by an increasing number of European immigrants who were not of English or Irish descent. After an agreement with international refugee organisations, 85,000 immigrants travelled to Australia in 1947-8 alone. Within a few years, Australia had over 100,000 new residents whose first language was not English. These new citizens brought new ideas with them. New styles of cooking, for example, led to welcome alternatives to the tedium of English cuisine. Their contribution helped Australia break out of its geographical isolation, to lessen the 'tyranny of distance'. In 1956, Melbourne became the first Australian city to host the Olympic games. In the year 2000, the games will return to the continent, this time to Sydney. Once more the eyes of the world will be turned toward Australia.

The First Australians

Europeans are, in fact, newcomers to Australia. Ages before the idea of Europe even existed, the first settlers had made the land their home. The first aboriginal peoples arrived in Australia at least 40,000 years ago. Over the millennia the population had to adapt to significant climatic change. At the time of the arrival of the first Europeans, aborigines had settled every region of the continent. Given this great span of time, it is not surprising that the culture the white people encountered was by no means monolithic. The Europeans, blind to any diversity, regarded the aborigines as savages, almost animals, living, without the benefit of religion, in unspeakable poverty. This viewpoint is now understood to have been a product of the Europeans' ignorance and prejudice. Aboriginal society was in fact highly organised, ordered by extremely supple and complex kinship ties and a deep religiosity.

Part of the reason for this profound misunderstanding was that the value systems of both peoples were in many ways diametrically opposed. The aborigines were highly successful hunters and gatherers. Their standard of living, at least as measured in terms of daily nourishment, was probably higher than most nineteenth-century Europeans. And they were able to sustain this with far less labour, perhaps as little as three days of work per week. Possessiveness was an unknown vice; the small bands that formed the primary social units were imbued with an ethos of sharing. When sufficient food had been procured, work stopped, leaving leisure time for religious and ceremonial pursuits. Probably most incomprehensible to the Europeans was the aborigines' relationship to the land. Though seemingly nomadic, their worldview was based on an affiliation with the landscape that had been passed down from father to son for untold eons. The ancestors had established this special spiritual relationship in the Dreamtime, the mythic period of creation during which the land and its animal and human inhabitants were born. Thus each family and each individual was indissolubly linked to specific places;

Two thousand metres long, the Great Barrier Reef is the largest coral reef in the world. Scientists believe that it is has been in existence for 15,000 years.

When the heat in Cairns becomes too oppressive, residents holiday in Kuranda. The train station of this picturesque town is set in a tropical garden.

World War II, aborigines were virtual prisoners in state-run reserves.

The 1930s saw the birth of the aboriginal protest movement. Though this was derailed by the onset of World War II, it resumed with greater vigour in the 1950s, and then in many respects paralleled the civil rights movement in America. This movement had two main goals, which were sometimes at odds with each other. The first was to obtain equal protection under the law and full civil rights. The second was to recover the cultural identity of the people. Progress has been slow, but indisputable.

There are many accomplishments in which this nation, started a little over two hundred years ago by soldiers and convicts, can rightly take pride. In 1988, the Aussies celebrated the bi-centennial, the two hundreth anniversary of the founding of the prison settlement on the shores of the Bay of Sydney. Darker memories, however, cast a shadow upon the celebrations. Critics claim to see vestiges of the white settlers' early antagonism toward an aboriginal population that, in many ways, still leads a marginal existence. Land rights remain, to this day, one of the main areas of contention. The task of balancing conflicting interests in an equitable fashion is not an easy one, and it is one the country continues to grapple with, as it enters into what most Australians hope will be a more honourable chapter in their history.

these were their patrimony and their responsibility.

The meeting of two such divergent cultures was inevitably destined to have tragic consequences. As throughout the rest of the colonised world, the arrival of the white man resulted in the near total destruction of the way of life of the indigenous people. In the beginning, tensions broke out in armed conflict, though disease depleted the aboriginal population more than actual warfare. Once the Europeans had firmly established their dominance, quasi-legal, though no less effective, means of population control were instituted. Chief among these were resettlement, child removal and forced assimilation. By the end of the nineteenth century and up to the beginning of

Fauna and Flora

"I saw myself this morning," begins Cook's diary entry for June 24, 1770 "a little way from the Ship, one of the animals before spoke of; it was of a light mouse Colour and the full size of a Grey Hound, and shaped in every respect like one, with a long tail, which it carried like a Grey hound: in short, I should have taken it for a wild dog but for its walking and running, in which it jump'd like a Hare or Deer." Today we can immediately identify this animal, which seemed so curious to European eyes, as the kangaroo. Cook did not, however, note down one of the prime characteristics of the kangaroo — that their young, who are more helpless than other mammals at birth, are carried in their mother's pouch. The kangaroo, a member of the marsupial order, is a vestige from the prehistoric era and was able to survive relatively unchanged through the eons of Australia's isolation. In the past, there existed kangaroos as large as rhinoceroses; today the red kangaroo is the largest example of its race. This species of kangaroo was unknown to Cook and his contemporaries, because it dwells in the interior. Cook's diary entry refers to the large grey kangaroo that frequents the eucalyptus forests and for this reason can be seen on the coasts. The grey kangaroo, like all of its family, is herbivorous.

The kangaroo family comprises the smaller wallaroos, the antelope kangaroos, different varieties of tree-climbing kangaroos, and the small rat kangaroos. Often confused with kangaroos are the wallabies, of which there are twenty-seven species on

The farms of north Queensland are isolated and widely scattered.

the continent. Wallabies are found mainly in the rocky outback. They can reach the size of large dogs, are plant eaters, and are quite vulnerable to climatic variations.

Hunting the Kangaroo

Many tourists come back from Australia disappointed at not seeing kangaroos hopping through the wild. But there is no shortage of them, which is a chief cause of complaint for farmers. Left unchecked, kangaroos and related species overgraze the pastureland reserved for sheep and cattle. They also cause damage by knocking down fence posts. For these reasons, the farmers persistently lobby to increase the hunting quotas. Permission is granted when particular regions are threatened with overpopulation.

The reaction to such policies is usually swift. Animal protection leagues organise international campaigns. Articles appear with such headlines as 'Australians are hunting the kangaroo to the verge of extinction.' For the most part these concerns are overstated; there are, however, some species that do need to be protected.

Those hunting kangaroos have to obey strict laws. But in the wide-open territories, where there is deep resentment toward these animals that compete for scarce resources, farmers often do not adhere to them. Cases are known of locals, after a few beers in the pub, driving at night into the bush with their lights on. The kangaroos, blinded by their headlights, are easy targets. Paul Hogan's character in the movie *Crocodile Dundee* battles against this wholesale butchery. In one scene he surprises some of these 'hunters'. He sets one of the murdered kangaroos upright, hides behind him and, shining his headlights, shoots back with his own shotgun. The drunks, thinking that the kangaroos are firing on them, scatter in panic.

Kangaroos are practically inedible, except for their fleshy tails that are used for dog food. Business ventures that have tried to promote kangaroo meat as high in protein have been unmitigated failures. Although kangaroo meat poses no health risk, there was a nasty scandal a few years ago, when it was discovered that Australian beef exported to America had been mixed with the much cheaper kangaroo meat.

Inspiration for the Teddy Bear

One export article that is highly in demand is a tree-dwelling marsupial: the koala. This comical creature, which like the kangaroo can only be found on the sixth continent, is also known as the koala bear. That designation, though biologically incorrect, is understandable. With its grey, furry face, button eyes and snub nose, it resembles nothing so much as the teddy bear. As cuddly as they seem, these animals can do a lot of harm with their sharp claws. For this reason zookeepers give them stuffed koalas to grab, before they allow tourists to have their pictures taken with them. No zoo between Sydney and Perth can succeed without some of these animals. Affection for them seems boundless. This is why they

The coastal region of northern Queensland is known for its dense rainforest and extensive sugar plantations.

The Whitsunday Island Archipelago lies halfway between Brisbane and Cape York. There are seventy-four islands in the chain.

400,000 koalas living in the wild, while some decades ago there were a few million. Development and clearing practices are infringing on their habitat, and infectious diseases are rendering females infertile. These trends are extremely worrisome to those who are working to protect the population. Recently, well-funded programmes have been directed toward quarantining healthy animals to prevent these infections from spreading. Special laws have been enacted, forbidding the hunting of koalas. As early as 1927, koalas found themselves on the verge of extermination by hunters after their fine pelts. Breeding refuges were then established in places such as Phillip Island, and these have somewhat relieved their plight.

Phillip Island, near Melbourne, has grown into a successful nature preserve. The rocks that surround the island are home to a large colony of sea lions. They are drawn to the area because of the abundance of prey. The island is used as a breeding ground for a species of small penguin, and has become a popular tourist attraction. Every evening, after the hunt for food is over, the birds form ranks in what is a veritable penguin parade. Under the watchful eyes of park rangers, visitors can observe this daily ritual from a kind of grandstand. The penguins gather together at the water's edge in large groups and waddle just a few yards past the grandstand to their caves. It sometimes happens that, just as they are about to reach their destination, one of the penguins takes fright, and then the whole troop flies off in wild excitement back to the sea.

are in great demand, and zoos throughout the world are willing to trade rare species for them.

Despite the popularity of koala bears, the Australian government is extremely tight-fisted in granting export licences. Stringent protections are needed, since they are not hardy animals and are susceptible to all kinds of diseases. Moreover, they are very finicky eaters, consuming only the leaves of certain eucalyptus trees. Eucalyptus oil may be poisonous to some animals, but koalas thrive on it. They smell like huge eucalyptus lozenges; their pores exude it, and this keeps them free from parasites.

There is heated debate among biologists about conservation efforts on behalf of the koalas, since they are considered an endangered species. Today there are about

Many of the intensely coloured flowers that grow in the rainforests can be found only in Australia.

Green Politics

Concern for the ecology of places like Phillip Island is no longer confined to a handful of activists. In recent years, environmentalists have garnered widespread popular support and have entered into the political mainstream. The realisation that the landscape the Europeans found on first arriving was vanishing, or being transformed beyond all recognition, convinced people that strong action had to be taken. In 1989, American scientists reported that the hole in the ozone layer above Antarctica had widened to encompass Australia and New Zealand. At the same time, activists in Tasmania were able to halt the construction of a highly controversial hydroelectric plant. This success carried over to the voters, and in the next election, the environmentalists won seats in the Tasmanian parliament for the first time. Younger people have been influenced by the pro-environmental stands of rock stars, such as Peter Garret of the group 'Midnight Oil'.

These developments caused traditional politicians to take notice. In 1990, the then-Prime Minister, Bob Hawke, announced the launching of what he proclaimed as the most all-embracing environmental programme in the world. As a sign of his seriousness, he appointed Sir Ninian Stephen, former Governor-General for the Commonwealth, as Ambassador for the Environment, a post equal to that of a Cabinet minister. As part of the Ambassador's portfolio, he assumed responsibility for taking strong action against soil erosion and for planting over a million trees and bushes. Support was mobilised in the effort to repair the damage done to the world's ozone layer and to protect endangered species of plants and animals.

A special effort was reserved for rescuing the diminishing numbat population. This small animal, which eats about 20,000 ants a day, and for this reason is also called the anteater, is reduced at present to an estimated population of only 2,000. Foxes threaten the species with utter extinction. The state of Western Australia has now initiated a breeding programme for numbats at the Perth Zoo. It was no easy task for the zoo to come up with a suitable menu for their guests. 20,000 ants per day, per numbat, proved an insurmountable challenge. They had to develop a special diet consisting of milk, eggs and vitamins, and a generous portion of termites added for flavour, to win the numbats' approval.

Similar programmes are being considered for the wombat, but the threats they face are different. Wombats are big, and strong and plump. They can weigh as much as 65 lbs, and grow to a height of three feet. They have few natural enemies, and when danger threatens they hide in their underground burrows. But the population has been ravaged by disease spread by foxes and wild dogs. This has led biologists to build quarantine stations for them as well.

An Egg-laying Mammal

Also of great concern is another unusual animal that is found only in Australia, the duckbilled platypus. When news first came to Europe about this species, scientists thought it was an imaginary creature. The notion of an egg-laying mammal was considered preposterous. But the platypus does indeed exist. It is one to two feet in length, and looks like a curious cross between a beaver and a duck. It resembles the latter with its beak and webbed feet, and the former with its fur and broad rudder-like tail. The females of the species lay only two or three eggs each year. The young suck on their mothers' bellies — the milk comes directly through the skin, as the platypus does not have nipples. The platypus lives in caves by freshwater streams on the southeast coast of Australia and eats insects and insect larvae. It spends most of its time in the water but is happiest when the water is clean and fresh. Because of the growing water pollution in the highly populated

areas that surround its habitat, many Australians fear for its future.

The platypus has another unique feature. As one of the only surviving monotremes, its body structure hearkens back to prehistoric times. It has only one hind orifice, which serves both reproductive and excremental functions. There is one other mammal that resembles the platypus — the spiny, snub-nose echidna. It also lays eggs and only lives in Australia. The echidna's favourite food is termites. It uses its strong claws to break open termite mounds, and then its long slippery tongue penetrates the tunnels and crevices to snare its dinner. Both of these primordial animals are hardly ever met with in the wild; only trained observers can hope to detect them. Most game parks, however, have specimens

Raindrops bejewel the leaves of a eucalyptus.

This eucalyptus tree is set off against the red rocks of the countryside near Kununurra in Western Australia.

of the echidna and aquaria for the platypus wherein they can be viewed.

Another witness to the prehistoric age is the crocodile. It has also been under threat, but thanks to an enormous effort at preservation, its population has rebounded. Since the release of the film *Crocodile Dundee*, it has become a kind of unofficial mascot for the Australian tourist industry, at least in the Northern Territory and Queensland. Since this movie has been shown around the world, the demand for bush tours through the tropical areas of northern Australia has risen dramatically. Two kinds of crocodiles populate the northern waters: one, the Johnson crocodile, with its long, thin and straight snout, inhabits fresh water and is of no danger to humans. The other variety is the estuary crocodile. This species prefers salt water. The Australians, who are generally fond of nicknames, call them 'salties'. They are man-eaters and can reach up to 21 feet in length.

Snakes and Dingoes

There are creatures other than crocodiles to be careful about when swimming off the north coast of Australia. In certain seasons one may encounter sea wasps, a deadly poisonous variety of jellyfish. And of course, one ought not to overlook the sharks that surround the continent in great numbers. In addition there are over twenty species of poisonous water snakes to be found in coastal waters, though most of these, like their cousins on land, will flee at the approach of humans and only attack if they feel threatened. There are approximately 110 species of snakes in Australia, of which about sixty are poisonous. Those who venture into the outback will sometimes come across their traces, but living specimens are rarely met with. The same holds true for the dingoes. Sheep farmers report that these feral dogs attack their herds, but biologists disagree, insisting that dingoes primarily cull the sick and aged from the flocks. In 1981, the curious case of Lindy Chamberlain made headlines throughout Australia. She, along with her husband Michael, an Adventist minister, had been on a camping vacation in the Northern Territory when they reported that their nine-month old daughter Azaria was missing. They claimed that a dingo had, in their absence, dragged her off from a tent in which they were camping. The courts did not, however, believe them. They found that the evidence pointed to the parents having killed their own child, and they were both sentenced to life imprisonment. Six years later, a court of appeals reviewed the case, overthrew the ruling of the lower court and set the couple free. Hollywood made *A Cry in the Dark*, a film about this strange episode, with Meryl Streep in the starring role.

Biologists insist that dingoes are afraid of humans. One would require the services of a highly experienced guide, or extraordinary luck, to spot a dingo in the wild.

The Laughing Bird

Far easier to find in the outback are many of Australia's eight hundred species of birds. Over five hundred of these are thought to be indigenous to Australia. Many of these — the cockatoo, for example — congregate in great flocks, which flutter around remote farmsteads in great white or red clouds. Less frequently met with are emus. These ostrich-like birds have earned the antipathy of farmers, since they tear up the fences that stand in the way of their free wandering. Even though they are considered to be a kind of national bird, they are not very popular. Then there is the case of what is, without a doubt, the happiest creatures on the sixth continent, the kookaburras. Most Aussies would like them to disappear altogether. This bird, which is a part of the kingfisher family, is known for its characteristic loud laugh, a sound that resonates throughout the tropic

regions of the country and that has driven many sound sleepers to the brink of chronic insomnia. Nonetheless, many Australians admit that the kookaburra should rightly be considered the country's national bird.

The Acacia and the Eucalyptus

If animals belong on Australia's coat of arms, it is its abundant plant life that supplies the colour. Australian athletes wear green and yellow in international competitions, although the national flag with the Southern Cross and British Union Jack is dark blue, red and white. Many Australians, however, would like to change this design, and most seem to want a green and

The knotty forms of these dying trees— here on a flooded plain near Lake Argyle — are reminiscent of much of the continent's vegetation.

yellow flag. Two representative species of plants suggest these colours: the eucalyptus with its full green leaves, and the acacia with its bright yellow flowers. The acacia can be found throughout the continent in over 650 varieties. Most common is the wattle tree, whose blooms are the country's official flower.

Acacia can be met with in all the regions and climatic zones of Australia. They take so many forms, however, that it is often difficult for the layperson to recognise them. There are as many variations in their colour as there are in the forms of their leaves. Some types have fine, feathery leaves; others strong, large stalks. There is also a great variation in height among the different kinds of acacia (from small bushes to tall trees). Biologists are understandably intensely interested in the acacia; very few large plant species show such pronounced formal variation.

There are somewhat fewer species of the other typical Australian plant, the eucalyptus. Scientists have so far identified approximately four hundred and fifty. of them. Once, these trees were highly prized because of their aromatic oil, but today a much cheaper chemical substitute can be created in the laboratory. In Australia, these trees are called gum trees. Some varieties seem to peel themselves, and then their white stems reflect the sunlight. For the most part, eucalyptus trees grow to great heights, some to almost four hundred feet. Many of these grand trees have been cut down since the Europeans settled the continent, but some specimens remain to this day. The karri tree, a species found in the southern part of Western Australia, can

easily grow to a height of three hundred feet.

Even though the acacia and eucalyptus are quite striking, the plants native to Australia do not, in general, exhibit the wide variety seen in the animal kingdom. There are, nonetheless, some very unusual species of plants, such as the grass tree. This plant lives for hundreds of years but only grows to a height of twenty feet. Thus it seems to grow no more than one inch per year.

That this extraordinary plant has captured the interest of scientists makes sense. Often overlooked are the many species of toxic plants that are native to Australia. Field studies have established that most of these were well known to the aboriginal people, who even made use of them in hunting and fishing. They would, for

In one of Melbourne's many parks, Fitzroy Gardens, stands the picturesque Captain Cook's Cottage. This building was transported to Australia from the famous seaman's home in Yorkshire.

Ferdinand von Muller planted and landscaped the Royal Botanic Gardens in Melbourne in the nineteenth century. They are considered to be among the most beautiful gardens in the world.

Commerce in Australia

"This entire people is obsessed with amassing riches," observed Charles Darwin after a visit to Australia. "Even in the highest levels of society wool and livestock form the primary topics of conversation." In fact, these remarks very well describe the situation of the country in the 1830s when Darwin visited it. Finally, after decades of hardship, the young colony had begun to glimpse the possibility of prosperity. And this was all on account of a common domestic animal, the sheep, or to be precise the merino sheep. Other breeds were brought into Australia with the first prison transports, but they did not adapt well to the climate and required too much care to be commercially exploited.

That merinos arrived in Australia was, in fact, due to chance. And that they were to form the basis of the economy was thanks to one of the shadiest figures in Australian history. It all began with a royal gift, but not one given to Australia or its imperial masters in London. King Charles IV of Spain presented the Dutch crown with two rams and four ewes. Their progeny enriched the livestock holdings of the director of the East India Company in Cape Town. In 1797, two British vessels en route to the prison colony landed at the Cape of Good Hope, where the governor had just recently died. His widow offered the ship captains twenty-six merinos.

The officers, recognising a good investment, bought the entire herd, and brought them to Australia. Some did not survive the long sea voyage through the Indian Ocean, but those that did paid for the trip. One of

example, bait pools with some of these plants, thereby stunning the fish and making them easier to catch. The leaves of the pituri plant, which contains nicotine, can be chewed on and, in the correct dosage, are a mild stimulant. Needless to say, they can be fatal if taken in higher amounts. There are also a number of poisonous species that have been brought into Australia. Many of these are quite familiar, though not everyone realises that they can be harmful. These include the oleander and certain varieties of lily that are found in many Australian gardens. Many plants have been brought to Australia from Europe and, to a lesser extent, from Asia and the Americas. This holds true especially for common varieties of grains, fruits and vegetables.

A typical house in Hobart, the capital of Tasmania. After Sydney, it is the oldest city in Australia.

England's Larder

Even more difficult was the position of Australia's cattle ranchers. With its dense population, England generated a huge demand for beef and mutton. But the problem was satisfying that demand. How could meat and other perishable goods survive the weeks-long journey back to the mother country without spoiling? The answer was to await the development of modern refrigeration techniques. Then Australia and its neighbour New Zealand would be in the position to become the primary suppliers of meat for Great Britain.

Wool, meat and agricultural produce today count for the most valuable sector of Australia's export market. About 160 million sheep, of which three quarters are merino, live in Australia. And even though only a small fraction of the country's total landmass is rich enough for intensive cultivation, that part produces an average of 26 million tons of grain annually. In all, Australia exports almost two-thirds of its agricultural production. Growers can look back upon an almost 150 year tradition of supplying Great Britain, which was Australia's largest customer until recently. Now that has changed, due in part to new restrictions placed on the import of food by the European Community. Great Britain and the rest of Europe remain major customers, but now Australia also looks to Japan, China, the United States, Russia and the Arab states of the Middle East. Australia is currently the world's largest exporter of live sheep. Russia and China import significant quantities of wool, thereby bolstering Australia's pre-eminence in the international

the business partners was John Macarthur (whose career has already been briefly discussed), who established the first merino sheep ranch in Australia. Seeing that the breed was thriving in Australia, he purchased many more from Cape Town and shipped them back to New South Wales. The merino wool, which soon reached the markets of London, proved to be of exceptional quality and brought a tidy profit. Australia had found its first export commodity, one that could easily weather the long journey back to European markets. With other farm products, success was not so easy to come by. Various grains shipped from England did not do well on Australian soil. It took a number of years before plant breeders could develop varieties that would flourish in Australia's climate.

wool markets. It is also among the leading nations worldwide in its exports of beef, grain and sugar.

Australia's rich soil does not only yield grain, sugar cane and vegetables. The flat, dry surface of the continent encloses vast reserves of mineral wealth as well. All areas of the country share in this endowment. There is iron ore in the Pilbara region in the northern part of Western Australia, lead and copper mines in Mount Isa in Queensland, and uranium in Roxby Downs in South Australia. Almost all valuable minerals can be found in Australia in some quantity, from bauxite, tungsten and nickel, to glittering deposits of gold. Mineral exports add to up to billions of dollars annually. The search for the last of these, the nineteenth century 'gold rush', transformed the Australian economy and brought it unimagined material prosperity. Today, gold is the second most important mineral export, lagging only behind iron ore.

From Gold to Coal

Less spectacular than the story of gold is that of coal, which has nonetheless played a significant role in the growth of the Australian economy. Coal was first discovered in 1791, only three years after the first settlers arrived, in the vicinity of Sydney. Along with wool it was exported early on. In 1801, a ship laden with coal set sail for the British colony of India, and from there travelled to the Cape of Good Hope. The demand at this time, however, was not great. For that reason, the coal deposits,

although conveniently located near the coast of New South Wales, were not seriously exploited. Soon, however, the advent of steamships and steam-powered locomotives, would usher in a new industrial age that would make coal the original 'black gold', a highly sought after material. Now, coal mines led the way in the industrial growth of the continent. They also became an important part of the social and political landscape, and a testing ground for labour reform. In 1876, a commission, convened to scrutinise mining practices, established a fifty-hour working week for youths between the ages of thirteen and eighteen. At the same time, laws were enacted that prohibited women and children under thirteen from working in the mines.

Hobart is a particularly handsome city. It is known for its well-preserved examples of historic architecture.

Sign of the Big Lobster on the side of the highway. The coasts of Australia are a paradise for seafood lovers.

The Quest for Oil

With the closing of the Steam Age, coal was replaced by oil as a primary fuel. In Australia, just as in the rest of the world, coal dropped in value. Nonetheless, because of Japan's emergence onto the world stage and its acute lack of mineral wealth, the Australian coal industry retained at least one major customer. Until the beginning of World War II, Japanese steel works remained closely dependent upon supplies of coal from down under. Still, the captains of Australian industry were well aware of the increasingly important position of oil in the new world economy, especially after the end of the war. Despite its vast mineral riches, Australia seemed to lack large oil deposits. Geolo-

gists did not rule out the possibility that a major find was waiting to be discovered, but for a long time explorations proved fruitless. A well was finally drilled on the coast of Victoria, but it produced no more than a barrel of oil a day.

It was not until 1961 that a well dug near Moonie, in the outback of Queensland, began to produce oil in sufficient quantity to be commercially viable. But neither this nor other sites opened during this period produced any really significant amounts of oil. Today only one area, the straits between the Australian landmass and Tasmania, can lay claim to major oil production. It accounts for approximately 90% of the total Australian output. Because of this, Australia is, by and large, self-sufficient as far as oil is concerned and even has a modest amount left over for export. Many believe that more oil waits to be discovered, but the enthusiasm for exploration waxes and wanes in response to the price of oil. Its relative abundance during the '90s has discouraged investors from funding potentially risky searches. Recently Australia has begun to exploit its natural gas reserves, with which it is well endowed, and this is already paying rich dividends.

Diamonds and Opals

What riches still slumber undisturbed deep within the soil is illustrated by the success story of northern Australia. The hugely expensive Ord River scheme, which was begun in the 1960s, was meant to have created new farmland. To this end a dam was built on Lake Argyle to create the largest man-made lake in Australia. This was to provide water for a vast agricultural area around the newly created town of Kununurra. The ambitious project has been completed, but although there is now no shortage of water, the dream of making the desert blossom has not been fully realised. The extreme heat, inhospitable to many varieties of plants, and the distance from major markets, in part account for the fact that only a portion of this wide area is currently being cultivated. But there has been another more lucrative result of this vast project. During the 1970s, a geological survey concluded that this area might very well harbour precious stones. Today, the Argyle diamond mines produce more diamonds than any other mine in the world. In fact, they account for 36% of the world diamond supply — 6% of this total is of the first quality, 39% is of second quality, while the balance is of industrial grade. These diamonds are used for drill bits and other purposes that call for extremely hard surfaces. A second mining complex was opened nearby in the late 1980s. Shortly after its inception, it had already achieved a production total of 625,000 carats per annum.

In regards to semi-precious stones, the opal plays the most important role by far in the Australian economy. Good opals are almost as expensive as diamonds (especially black opals, which are only found in the Lightning Mountains in New South Wales). However, unlike diamonds, there are no industrial uses for opals. This highly desirable gemstone, which is most frequently milky-white, shot through with grains of colour, is found mainly in inhos-

pitable regions, where towns built around the mines such as Coober Pedy, Amberooka and Andamooka have sprung up. For this reason the search for opals can be a kind of crapshoot, in which one can be instantly rich, or labour fruitlessly for a lifetime.

Opals have been particularly good for the tourist business. Stores offering a wide selection of fine opals can be found in every major city. Some stores are so dependent on tourists that they offer free pick-ups by limousines from good hotels. The visitor will find most jewelers to be quite helpful. They will explain the wide variations in the quality of the stones. Opals are categorised by size, density, and the strength of the colours that add to their unique translucent effect.

The explorer Matthew Flinders (1774-1814) gave Kangaroo Island its name. Still today many of these fascinating creatures live there.

Nomads of the New Age

The success that opals have had in the last decades is due in large measure to the upsurge in tourism. This phenomenon has resulted in a concentrated effort to promote the service sector of the economy. Up until the 1960s, tourism had little role to play in this land so far off the well-worn paths of vacation routes. According to the Bureau of Statistics, there were on average 475,000 visitors to Australia in the years 1971-1975. By 1990, this number had surpassed the two million mark. And with the arrival of the 2000 Olympic games, Australia is bracing itself for an even greater number. Today, tourism has nearly overtaken mining and the exploitation of raw materials as the leading industry in the land. When the price of commodities on the world markets decreases, tourists become all the more important.

The tourist market, as travel agents very quickly learn, does present its own difficulties and dangers. It does not fluctuate with the commodity markets, except that it is linked to some extent to the price of oil. But it is dependent on changes in currency valuations and, as the effects of the recent economic slowdown in Asia brought home, especially subject to the influence of macro-economic conditions. Then there are traits in the Australian character that have to be reckoned with. Among these is a seeming fondness for labour disputes. In 1989, for example, airline pilots went on a month-long strike. This had a crippling effect on the entire industry, not only because Australia lies so far from most of the countries from which the tourists come, but also because travelling by air is the most efficient way to see the country. Travellers from abroad want to visit Ayers Rock and the Great Barrier Reef, but their inaccessibility by means other than air transport makes a smoothly-functioning airline system all the more important. As a consequence, many travel agents discouraged groups from making the trip to Australia that year. The financial loss was severe, but even greater was the damage to the country's image in foreign eyes. "Strikes in distant lands have almost as chilling an effect on tourism as natural catastrophes," remarked one long-time travel agent. "It would be unfortunate if Australia were to develop a reputation as a strike-prone country."

Five Million Vacationers

The Canberra regime has sought, through the deployment of the military, to lessen the effects of strikes on the tourist industry, and this in itself shows how seriously the government regards its visitors from overseas. This was not always the case; only recently, has the national government recognised the importance of tourism. It was not until 1984, that an official report noting the positive effects of tourism on the economy signalled a shift in attitude.

Since then, tourism has grown to account for about six percent of the gross national product; along with technology, this sector remains the fastest growing part of the economy. It provides more jobs than the auto and textile industries put together. Plus, many of these jobs are in regions that otherwise provide few employment opportunities. The Australian Tourist Commission has a worldwide network of offices and is confident in reaching its goal of five million visitors per annum by the end of the year 2000. Particular attention is being paid to Australia's Asiatic neighbours. Now that the economic reversals of the mid-nineties seem to have been halted, Australia is once again reaching out to their upwardly mobile populations. If one includes visitors to New Zealand and Oceania, Asian tourists make up the largest share of overseas visitors. In second place are the Europeans, which is not surprising given the special relationship between Australia and Great Britain. American tourists, while smaller in numbers, usually spend more per capita on their vacations and accordingly, occupy a highly valued position in the calculations of the industry.

The tourist industry has served to galvanise the service sector of the Australian economy. Today almost three-quarters of the working population are employed in service industries. Two statistics demonstrate the importance of this. Of the approximately one million new jobs that were created in the 1980s, almost 98% of them were in the service sector. Service industries have become an increasingly important part of the global economy, and they have spread far beyond the confines of the tourist business. Overall, Australia's share of the worldwide service industry is small, but the government has come to realise that this is where Australia's future lies.

Gold has wrought more
changes to Australia
than any other
resource. In Kalgoorlie
in Western Australia
the "golden days" have
not entirely passed
away. There is still
one working mine,
while the others have
become popular tourist
attractions. Visitors
can pan for gold and
are sure to find some
gold dust.

The discovery of gold brought money to Kalgoorlie, and its buildings display this prosperity. Today, this richly ornamented historic town draws visitors from all over the world.

The Pinnacles on the
Australian west coast
create a landscape that
is as puzzling as it is
fantastic. Shaped by
erosion over thousands
of years, hundreds of
bizarre rock formations
rise out of the sand.

Only the license plate indicates that this photo was taken in Western Australia. It could just as easily have been shot in another part of the country.

"Road trains" are
an institution in
Australia. Heavy
trucks pull up to three
cars behind them
rumbling through the
country's open spaces.
Often the cargo areas
are two or three stories
high. They are mainly
used to transport sheep
and cattle.

*Australia's flora and
fauna have a wider
diversity than one
might suppose at first
glance. These huge trees
suck up moisture to
survive the long dry
season.*

Lake Argyle near Kununurra in Western Australia is the largest man-made lake in the country. It adds to the austere appeal of the landscape. But contrary to the hopes of its investors, it has not yet succeeded in drawing tourists in great numbers.

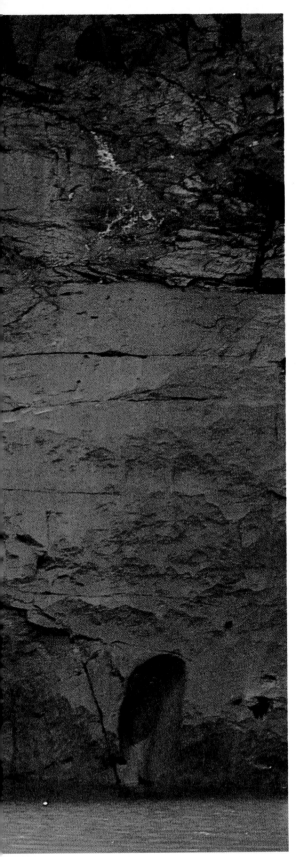

The reflection of the sky and the water of a small pond tinge a rock wall with blue in the sunshine in Kakadu National Park. The park is a mecca for ornithologists. It is home to about 250 different species of birds.

A strip of wetlands in Kakadu National Park created by floods from the Crocodile River in the rainy season. In the dry season, the remaining water holes become magnets for the park's abundant wildlife.

Colourful flowers, deep greens and high grasses are the hallmarks of the rainy season in the Northern Territory, but heavy flooding makes it difficult for the visitor to travel here at this time of year. Termites build earthworks several feet high to protect themselves from the rising waters.

A landscape at two different seasons: the clear blue sky and yellow grass of the dry season in the Northern Territory quickly changes colour, when the grey storm clouds that herald the approaching deluge dump heavy rains on the parched earth.

Aboriginal hand crafts are attentively preserved on Bathurst Island, which lies off the coast not far from the city of Darwin. The great demand for traditional pottery and textile design has improved economic conditions on the island.

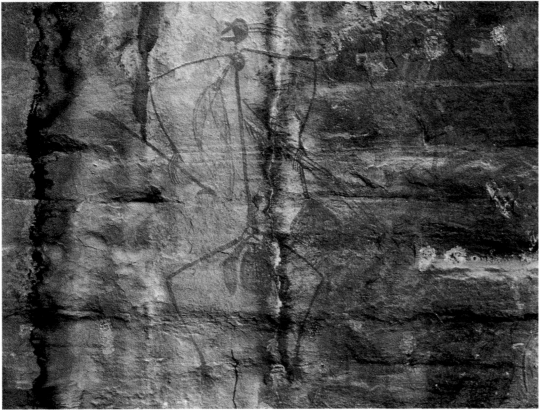

Bathurst and Melville Islands: A totemic statue carved from wood recalls those used in aboriginal ritual practices. A rock painting conveys an elemental expressiveness.

The colours of the rock walls in Katherine Gorge change during the course of the day. Depending on the angle of the sun, they can appear stone grey, bright orange or dusky red.

The impressive MacDonnell Ranges around Alice Springs stand out as a tremendous natural barrier in the heart of the country. Water holes in the mountains attract kangaroos. Here kangaroo crossing signs are not a curiosity, but a necessity.

Stanley Chasm in the MacDonnell Ranges in central Australia is nearly three hundred feet deep and at its narrowest point only ten feet wide. Sunlight illuminates the darkness here for only a short time each day. Above, an attenuated eucalyptus tree stands out against the backdrop of a cliff wall.

PRECEDING SPREAD:
For many the high point of a visit to Australia, Ayers Rock rises 348 metres above the surrounding plain. From a distance the rock looks relatively smooth, but as one gets nearer tortuous channels created over millennia by erosion and other geological forces become visible.

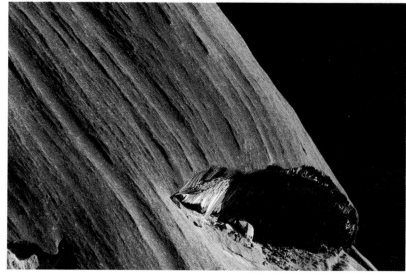

Ayers Rock has a circumference of about nine kilometres. It is a sacred place for the aborigines, whose name for it is Uluru. Today, it is the centre of a national park, which by treaty with the aborigines indigenous to this region, is administered jointly by the government and the tribes themselves.

FOLLOWING SPREAD:
Nearby Ayers Rock stand the Olgas. The valleys and streams that run through these low mountains are home to numerous species of wild animals.

Adelaide, the art-conscious capital of South Australia, is a more or less successful conglomeration of new and old buildings. The street plan for this city, which was founded in 1836, features broad boulevards that have proven to be well adapted for a city that is now home to over one million people.

The Botanic Gardens, with its impressive greenhouse, is host to a large number of exotic species of plants drawn from all over the continent.

Adelaide is rightly
proud of its support
of the arts and rivals
Sydney in this respect.
The Torrens Lake
Festival Centre, in
front of which this
modern sculpture
stands, offers artists
of all kinds ample
exhibition space.

Opposite ends of Australia: Sunset seen from Cape York, the northernmost tip of Australia, and Cape Willoughby Lighthouse on Kangaroo Island off its south coast.

This group of rocks on the shores of Victoria near Port Campbell are called the "Twelve Apostles". They are part of a national park that runs along the Great Ocean Road and includes a line of spectacular fjords.

The coastline of the
states of Victoria and
South Australia offer
many lovely scenic
overviews and are
filled with stark and
appealing contrasts.
Here are shown a strip
of Victoria's impressive
coast, the stark flat
land of Kangaroo
Island and a lightly
wooded area of euca-
lyptus out in the bush.

The sea lions on Kangaroo Island have long since become accustomed to the presence of tourists. Sometimes they even seem to pose for photographers. The presence of opals and skilled jewellers also draws tourism to the island.

PRECEDING SPREAD:
This rock formation on Kangaroo Island has been hollowed out by wind and water over thousands of years into a wavelike shape. Many natural monuments are protected here; over one fifth of the island is currently national park land.

*A typical Australian
scene, even if a bit
unusual for Tasmania,
which is more
mountainous than
flat. Nevertheless
sheep farming plays
as important a role
on Australia's largest
island as it does in the
rest of the country.*

Historic charm and
the skyscrapers of the
financial district,
which suffers from a
constant shortage of
office space, are the
hallmarks of
Melbourne. The
former is represented by
the old street cars and
the elaborate facade of
Flinders Street
Station, the latter by
the ever-growing
skyline.

The highly ornamented architectural style of Melbourne's central district offers small businessmen the opportunity to display their wares.

Misty days in May presage the arrival of autumn. Although the seasons are opposite those in the Northern Hemisphere, the temperatures are not comparable. In Melbourne there is seldom frost.

To find snow in Australia, one has to travel to high elevations. A favourite spot is Mount Buller in Victoria, which has become Australia's largest ski resort.

*Southwest Victoria
is Australia's richest
agricultural region.
Farming methods have
been perfected since the
first pioneers arrived.
Some techniques are
home-grown since
what worked in
Europe often did not
succeed down under.*

The Wild West in
Australia's East. In
Ballarat, a town that
was built during the
gold rush, the feel of
that earlier time has
been recreated. Actors
play the part of miners
and cowboys and a
shoot-out on Main
Street completes the
picture.

Australia's south coast, as this handsome residence indicates, has long been a desirable place to live. But the area has its share of scientific curiosities as well. Blue Lake still remains somewhat of a puzzle. For a month in summer its grey waters change overnight into a startling blue.

The British colonised Tasmania shortly after establishing a presence in Sydney. The island is a favourite vacation spot for Australians who find it familiar and exotic at the same time. Towns like Ross with old-fashioned architecture, like that of its charming Post Office, appeal to those interested in the country's history, while the deep green forest offers the feeling of a south sea island.

FOLLOWING SPREAD:
On a clear day passengers flying into Sydney are treated to a panorama of the city and the bay, including the Harbour Bridge and the flowing white roof of the Sydney Opera House.

Merry Old England in the heart of Sydney. Lawn bowlers don't let the noise and confusion of their surroundings interfere with their concentration on the game. Lawn bowling is practically a national sport; it's played in every region of the country.

Another view of Sydney, from north of the Harbour Bridge. Tourists don't frequent this district, since it lies at a distance from the attractions of the Bay.

Australia's largest city seen from its best side. The Opera House and Harbour Bridge and suburbs are illuminated by floodlights and the sinking sun. No wonder young couples find the harbour cruise at twilight so romantic.

"The finest piece of water I ever saw," so wrote Captain Arthur Phillip the founder of the city, on first beholding Broken Bay and Pittswater, two large bays to the north of Sydney. Today visitors come to surf and dive.

The symmetrical plan of the Australia's capital city, Canberra, is displayed in this photograph. One of the city's primary axes leads from the Australian War Memorial, down the tree-lined ANZAC Parade, across Lake Burley Griffin to the old and new Parliament Buildings. The New Parliament House was opened in 1988. The Australian flag waves over it.

Though the tennis players of today dismiss the sport's traditional dress code, lawn bowlers still adhere to the time honoured for-mulation and dress all in white. This makes good sense on Australia's Gold Coast, where the sun is a force to be reckoned with.

It is now rare to see ladies and gentlemen dressed in the old British fashion, especially at the beach. Here you can wear anything you want as long as you have a hat to protect yourself from the blazing sun.

Rapid economic development over the last thirty years has changed the face of Brisbane, Australia's third largest city. As a result, the old government house stands in the shadow of surrounding skyscrapers. Architectural values often seemed to have been overlooked in the midst of the construction boom. An unsightly example is the highway that runs right along the harbour.

Australia is home to a
wide diversity of plant
life. Giant ferns, like
those to the left grow-
ing on the Island of
Tasmania, flourish in
the cool rainy south;
whereas in the tropical
north one finds
specimens of orchids
and other exotic
flowers.

On a trip through Australia, the visitor may often experience a sense of deja vu. Above is a pub from Townsville. With its delicate facade, it could just as easily be standing in Tasmania, and the wind-swept landscape to the right, while set in Tasmania, recalls the countryside in Queensland.

Much of Australia is
largely untamed. Here,
the effects of nature can
be sharply felt. Floods
perennially trouble
this island continent.
Brush fires can also
cause great destruction,
though the facing
picture is of a
controlled fire set to
a sugar cane field.

Two faces of the Australian coast: Above, a surfer's paradise with Brisbane's skyline in the background. To the right, island harbours in the Whitsunday Archipelago, part of the Great Barrier Reef, offer sailors a tranquil retreat.

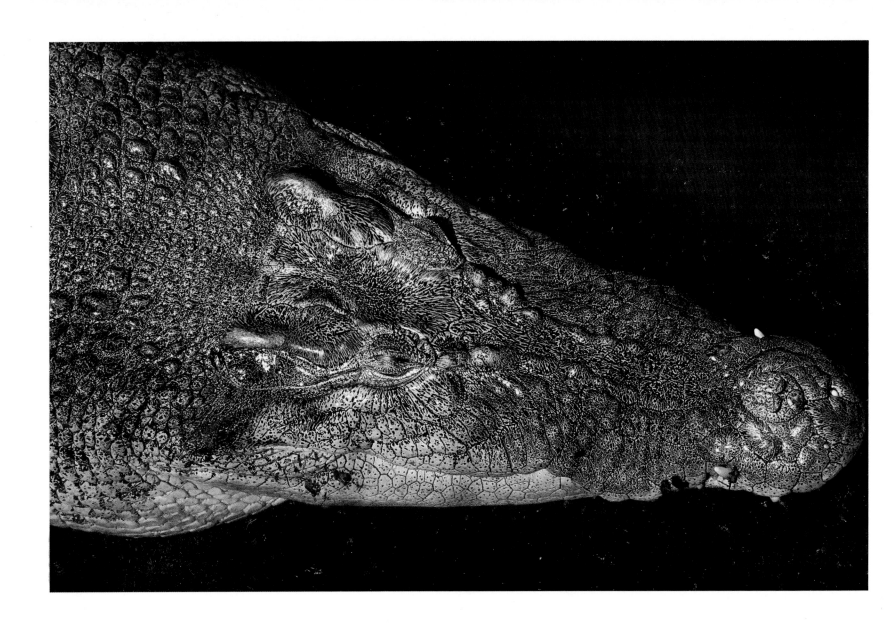

The irresistible koala is
not only the prototype
of the teddy bear but
the unofficial mascot
of Australia. But the
less affable crocodile has
challenged its
pre-eminent position
since the world-wide
success of the movie,
Crocodile Dundee.

The hanging roots of a great tree and the dramatic power of a waterfall curtain offer some sense of the diverse scenery in the unspoiled parks on the Atherton Tableland. This area, lying in the northern region of Queensland, is known for its extraordinary natural beauty.

"Bushies", as bush pilots are known, provide an extremely valuable service. Their often creaky planes are the only way of travelling to and supplying the farms and towns that dot remote and inaccessible areas of the country. Tourists can still treat themselves to a ride on some of these "old birds", such as the DC-3 pictured above.

When Australians talk
about the beach of their
dreams, they are
usually referring to
those in North Queens-
land. They are the most
frequented holiday
destination in the
country. But every
state has more than
its share of beautiful
sandy beach.

PRECEDING SPREAD:
*Australia has
thousands of miles of
coastline. The visitor
who explores some of its
countless coves and
inlets may feel as if he
has stumbled upon an
undiscovered land,
ornamented only by the
work of nature. This
photograph taken north
of Cairns in Queens-
land conveys some of
this natural beauty and
tranquillity.*

*The islands of the
Great Barrier Reef lie
in the astounding blue
of the Pacific like places
glimpsed in a dream.
Photography can only
hint at the richness of
the underwater world
that awaits the diver.*

Even in Queensland, which is known as the sunshine state, the weather has another side to it. The rolling grey clouds are not, however, altogether unwelcome, since they provide the rainfall that helps the plant life thrive on its many idyllic islands.

*"I'd rather be sailing,"
is one of Australians'
favourite sayings.
Given the glorious
coastline that rings the
continent—here are
pictured scenes from
Cairns and the Great
Barrier Reef—the
sentiment is entirely
understandable.*

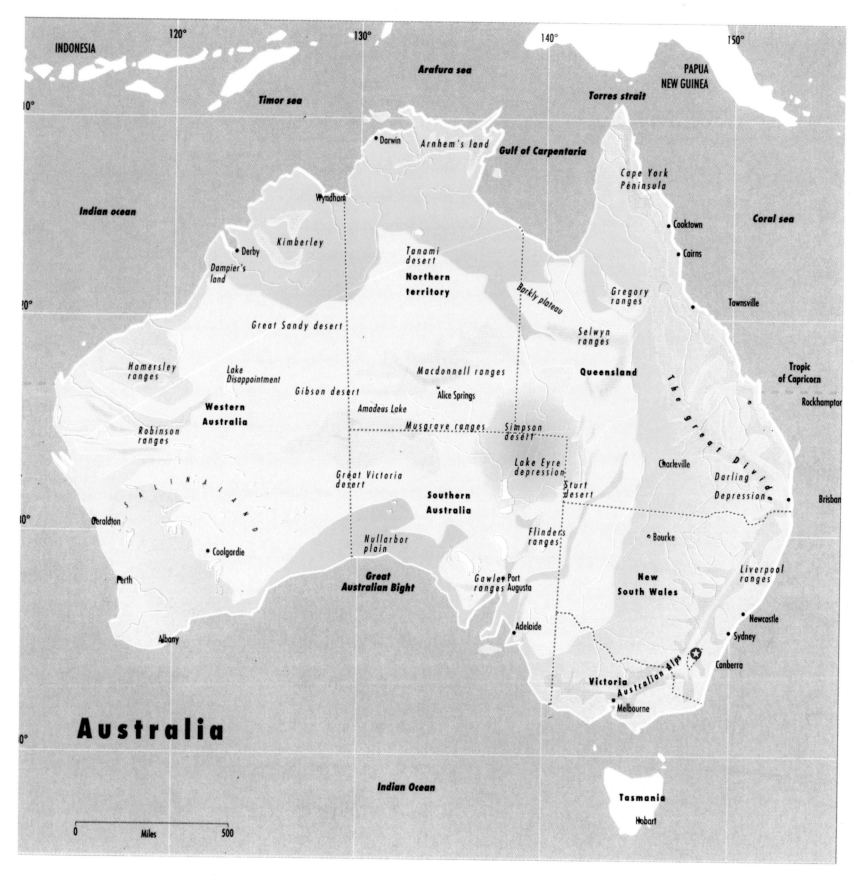

INDONESIA

120°

130°

140°

150°

Arafura sea

Timor sea

PAPUA
NEW GUINEA

Torres strait

10°

• Darwin   *Arnhem's land*

Gulf of Carpentaria

Indian ocean

*Cape York
Péninsula*

Coral sea

• Cooktown

Wyndham

Kimberley

• Derby

• Cairns

*Dampier's
land*

*Tanami
desert*

**Northern
territory**

Barkly plateau

*Gregory
ranges*

• Townsville

20°

Great Sandy desert

*Selwyn
ranges*

*Hamersley
ranges*

Lake
Disappointment

Macdonnell ranges

Queensland

*T
h
e
g
r
e
a
t
D
i
v
i
d
e*

**Tropic
of Capricorn**

Gibson desert

• Alice Springs

• Rockhampton

Amadeus Lake

**Western
Australia**

Musgrave ranges

*Simpson
desert*

*Robinson
ranges*

• Geraldton

S
A
L
I
N
A
L
A
N
D

*Lake Eyre
depression*

Charleville

*Darling
Depression*

• Brisban

*Great Victoria
desert*

**Southern
Australia**

*Sturt
desert*

30°

• Coolgardie

*Flinders
ranges*

• Bourke

*Nullarbor
plain*

**New
South Wales**

*Liverpool
ranges*

Perth

**Great
Australian Bight**

*Gawler
ranges*

Port
Augusta

Newcastle

Albany

• Adelaide

Victoria

Australian Alps

• Sydney

• Canberra

Australia

40°

Indian Ocean

• Melbourne

Tasmania

• Hobart

0   Miles   500

A Journey through Australia

Because of Australia's size and its distance from most of the world's capitals, you need to make some decisions before setting out. The first is how to get there. Then, once you arrive, the question becomes what to see and what to leave out. The answer will naturally depend on how much time you have allotted. For a stay of two weeks (anything less is impractical), you might plan an itinerary that includes Sydney, Alice Springs, Ayers Rock, the Great Barrier Reef and Brisbane. Stay an extra week and you can include Melbourne, Canberra and Adelaide. If you are fortunate enough to have more time at your disposal, you can travel to Tasmania in the south, Perth in the west, or Darwin, in the tropical northern region of the continent.

Sydney

Almost every major metropolitan centre in Australia has an international airport, but the majority of visitors land in Sydney. This inviting city, home to 3.5 million inhabitants, is the largest in Australia. It is the capital of New South Wales and a high point of any trip to the continent. Its residents can rightly take pride in its beautiful natural harbour, with its numerous coves and inlets, its many parks and nature preserves, and lovely residential areas. "God made the harbour and saw that it was good, but the devil made Sydney," so said Mark Twain. And though he might have had some justification for this observation in the late nineteenth century, today Sydney is spoken of in the same breath as San Francisco, Hong Kong and Rio de Janeiro.

There is no doubt that Sydney was an unwelcoming place for the first European arrivals, who laboured to carve out a settlement from the surrounding wilderness. The deportees had a hellish time of it: hunger and disease, heat and continual hostilities with the aboriginal population whose land they were usurping, characterised life in these early years. To be sent out to Australia was a severe punishment indeed. But today, Sydney is an altogether different place from the dilapidated barracks that housed the first unwilling settlers. Skyscrapers stand out against the immaculate blue of sea and sky and justify its claim to being the Manhattan of the South Seas. In the 1980s, the city profited from the wave of prosperity in Asia, and the Japanese in particular made major investments in real estate. Now after a temporary decline, property values are once again beginning to rise. Tourism is on the increase and an unprecedented number of visitors are expected for the 2000 Olympic games.

One of Sydney's great prizes is its splendid natural harbour; this is why the settlement was first established here. Captain Phillip observed on landing in Sydney Bay: "We have found the best harbour in the world." Visitors should take the ferry across its sparkling waters to the zoo, or to Manly, one of the lovely Pacific beaches that grace the city. Many ferry lines embark from Circular Quay in the city and make connections to Sydney's upscale suburbs, such as Watson Bay, which offers many fine seafood restaurants situated right on the bay. Another favoured destination is Double Bay. Because of its expensive boutiques the locals like to refer to it as 'Double Pay'.

The ferries offer a pleasant and inexpensive way to explore the harbour area. Somewhat more costly, however, are the tourist liners that circle the harbour — here you have the benefit of experienced guides; many also serve coffee in the afternoon, or candlelight dinners in the evening.

A general store in Sydney.

tower is a monorail that leads to Darling Harbour, a once-decaying industrial area that has been transformed into a vibrant commercial centre, with a convention site, shopping arcades with over two hundred stores and restaurants, an aquarium, and two museums — the National Maritime Museum and the Powerhouse Museum.

The Powerhouse Museum, named for the power station that once stood on this site, is the largest and one of the most interesting in the country. It combines the arts and sciences, and both social and technological history. There is, for example, a display of the primitive tools that were all the first Europeans had to create a livable settlement out of the wild lands surrounding them.

One of the most daunting challenges for the founders of Sydney was the need for

Commercial street through the centre of Sydney.

Photography buffs will certainly not want to miss the city's best-known landmarks — the Harbour Bridge, nicknamed 'the coathanger', and the famed Sydney Opera House, whose opening in 1973 marked a new era of cultural awareness for Australians. Prior to this, culture and the arts were deemed luxuries of little importance, and somehow not in line with the nation's rough-and-tumble way of life. At first, there were harsh words directed toward the new building, and critics objected to its great expense. But the costs of the project did not fall on the taxpayers. The construction was entirely financed by lotteries and fund raising from private sources. Even more galling to the rather conservative population was its daring architectural design. One wit dubbed it 'two turtles having sex', while other barbs were even more pointed. These so angered Jorn

Utzon, the Danish architect who won the commission, that he left Australia before his project was completed. And yet today, the Opera House has become a recognised emblem for the entire continent. The international acclaim for this striking piece of architecture with its sail-like roof encouraged an increased interest in culture and a willingness to lend financial support to the arts.

Not long after, the oldest part of Sydney, the Rocks, began to benefit from a major restoration. Eating places and fine shops sprang up in this once-languishing district, and soon, the main complaints were that it had grown too crowded with sightseers. Despite the throng of tourists, the visitor owes himself a visit to the 300-metre high Centrepoint Tower. It offers a splendid panorama of the city and its parks, the harbour and outlying areas. Right outside the

good pasturage and agricultural land. The search took them to the Blue Mountains, about 100 kilometres from the city. Today, trains and highways make getting to the mountains easy, but once there it is not hard to imagine how formidable a barrier they would have been in earlier times. Geological forces have cut deep ravines into the precipitous and heavily wooded cliff walls, and only a few years ago, it took weeks to recover the wreck of a small plane that had crashed there. Nonetheless, the Blue Mountains are now a favourite weekend-getaway spot for city dwellers, especially in January and February; while Sydney bakes in the heat of the Australian summer, they offer cool mountain breezes. Through these elevations winds the steepest mountain road in the world, once used to supply the mines. It ushers the visitor into a scenic valley where three rock outcroppings stand next to one another. These are known as the Three Sisters and, according to the aborigines, are endowed with mythological significance.

Canberra

It is about 300 kilometres from Sydney to Canberra, the capital of the Commonwealth of Australia. Even though the southeast coast is the most densely populated part of the country, once you leave the suburbs of Sydney behind, there is a distinct sense of wide-open spaces, especially if you avoid the Coast Highway and go inland on Highway 31 and 23. For those who don't wish to drive, the train offers a pleasant alternative. There are also frequent flights into Canberra Airport.

As political capital of the country, Canberra has had to contend with the rivalry between Sydney and Melbourne. Though

Canberra's National Library lies on the shore of Lake Burley Griffin.

not equidistant from them — it is about 650 kilometres from Melbourne — it is sufficiently far away to be out of each one's circle of influence. The founders of the capital established the Australia Capital Territory surrounding it (known as ACT) so that the city would be within its own political jurisdiction.

Canberra is an aboriginal word meaning 'meeting place', an appropriate term for a city in which the country's politicians gather (that the word is also used to denote a woman's breast is mentioned here only in passing). Canberra has also been called 'a suburb in search of a city', and 'the junk shop that ruined a good sheep field', among other things. These nicknames allude to the city's reputation as being a haven for boring bureaucrats, born out of a test tube. There is some truth to these remarks — half the city's

work force is on the government payroll, and one cannot help but notice a certain artificiality, not present in less carefully planned urban areas. But there are positives here as well. Canberra is the fastest growing city on the continent, with many people attracted to its park-like surroundings.

Canberra was officially declared the capital on March 12, 1913, but with a world war intervening, it was not until 1927 that the members of parliament were settled in their permanent home. Finally, in 1988, the city erected an impressive new Parliament House on Capital Hill, fulfilling the idea on which the city was founded. The plan for the city arose out of a worldwide competition, won by the American architect, Walter Burley Griffin. He envisioned two main districts separated by a man-made lake, with each district formed on a circular plan, and with

Hobart is famous for its charming old houses.

boulevards intersecting those radiating from the centre.

This plan can be recognised from a number of lookout points that surround the city. The widest views can be had from the 195-metre high television tower that has an observation deck and restaurant, and Black Mountain, which is over 800 metres high. But the whole of Griffin's concept can best be appreciated from the 842-metre high Mount Ainlie, behind the Australian War Memorial. From here, you can make out the axis that leads from the War Museum across the lake, to the old and new parliament buildings. On the parliament side of the lake stand the National Library, the Australian National Gallery and the High Court of Australia. Out of the lake rises a tower, with a carillon of 53 bells. Most Sundays, concerts are given that can easily be heard in the inner city. The impressive fountain of the Captain Cook Memorial spouts upward from the middle of the lake to a height of 140 metres, making it the tallest fountain in the world. Next to the new parliament building, Canberra's main attraction is the war memorial, dedicated to Australians who fell in the line of duty, and a connected war museum, an impressive, neo-byzantine style building with a copper dome.

Hobart

After stopping in Canberra, the traveller should pay a visit to the island of Tasmania off the southeast coast of the continent. Tasmania is the smallest state in the commonwealth, but it lives quite well from tourism. The tourism industry, next to fruit cultivation and forestry, is the most important source of income for Tasmania, and mainland Australians go there for vacations even if they only have a few days off. The island has many features that are difficult to come by on the mainland: a significant number of well-preserved architectural and historical sites, a climate that is pleasant almost all year round, and extensive wilderness areas.

The historical sites in Tasmania, as in the whole of Australia, are not old by European or even American standards. They, for the most part, recall the dark era of the penal colony. In 1642, the Dutchman, Abel Janszoon Tasman, the first European to set foot on the island, landed there thinking he had reached the mainland. In 1855, when the island was established as a colony, it was given the name Tasmania after its discoverer. The early nineteenth century was a melancholy period for Tasmania. The British colonial powers used it as an additional penal colony. The prison guards looked upon the aboriginal inhabitants of the island as an inferior race, living little better than animals. At times they even organised hunting parties to pursue the unfortunate native population like wild game. It only took a few decades for the British to wipe out the entire native population of the island, which is estimated to have been around 4,000.

The colonial government was not much gentler with the prison population, especially in the town of Port Arthur. Prisoners were treated decently as long as they caused no trouble to the authorities. Still, Port Arthur was feared and hated, because the labour was extremely hard; the guards were also known for their brutality, and the chance of escape was almost zero. Access by land was patrolled by guard dogs and protected with fences, and guardhouses contributed to the tight security. There were no ships to escape by sea, and those who tried to swim off the island had to contend with the sharks. The ruins of Port Arthur are still an impressive sight, and tens of thousands of visitors come to see it every year.

Provisions for the penal colony came from Hobart, Tasmania's capital, which was founded in 1804. In this small town there are more historical sites preserved than in the largest cities in Australia. Hobart was settled shortly after Sydney, and as such is the second-oldest city in the land. Within a small compass there is a great deal to see here. About one hundred buildings have been classified as historic landmarks by the national trust, especially those built in the Georgian style, out of sandstone or red brick. That is evidenced in the Battery Point district, which bears witness to the island's colonial past. The restored warehouses in Salamanca Place were built between 1838 and 1860; they offer a clear reflection of this period, as do St. George's Anglican Church, a good example of the colonial style of ecclesiastical architecture, and Arthur's Circus, a ring of fifteen Georgian buildings. Many of the old buildings in Battery Point have been converted to art galleries, boutiques and fine restaurants. During the summer months there is also an outdoor market.

Battery Point stands in the shadows of the artillery battery that was designed to protect the early settlement. In those early years, Tasmania played an important, strategic role for the colony on the mainland. The Anglesea Barracks, the oldest military base still in use, bears witness to this. Dating back to the same period are the Theatre Royal and the Cascade Brewery, each the oldest functioning example of its kind in Australia. Other impressive buildings are the Customs House, built in 1902, and its predecessor, which was begun in 1835 and now serves as Parliament House. It is not surprising that a city with so

Flinders Street Station, built in the style of the French renaissance, stands in the heart of Melbourne.

much history also has many museums. Van Dieman's Land Folk Museum is devoted to the life of Tasmania's pioneers. Nearby in the Tasman Maritime Museum, exhibits trace the history of the city and its sea-faring past, with special attention paid to the time of the great whalers. The Tasmanian Museum and Art Gallery specialises in the colonial epoch and also contains a collection of aboriginal artifacts. The Post Museum tells the story of the extraordinary signalling system that connected Hobart and Port Arthur.

Melbourne

The principal city of the state of Victoria is famous for its parks, which is not surprising since Victoria is known as the 'Garden State'. It is the most English city on the continent,

notwithstanding the skyscrapers that give the Melbourne skyline an American cast. It is a city of over three million people, situated on the Yarra River. One disadvantage is that the centre of the city does not face the water, even though Port Phillip Bay is larger than Sydney Harbour. But when John Batman settled here in 1835, he decided that it would be more secure inland than right on the coast. Soon after, then-Governor Bourke hired the land surveyor, Robert Hoddle, to lay out a planned city. The present residents of Melbourne have good reason to thank Hoddle. He bequeathed it broad boulevards and shady trees.

At the beginning, the city of Melbourne struggled to survive. But then, two nearly simultaneous events occurred that led to a period of explosive growth. In 1851, Victoria became a British colony. At about the same

An outing in Fitzroy Gardens, one of Melbourne's many lovely parks.

time, gold was discovered, and the ensuing gold rush quadrupled the city's population. Within a few years a truly Victorian city had sprung up in the wilderness. Parts of this first stage of development can still be seen and appreciated — the Royal Arcade, for example, an elegant promenade for shopping which opened its doors in 1869.

The city's fathers were blessed with foresight. They invested heavily in parks and laid the foundation for the beautiful Royal Botanic Gardens, which is now home to over 12,000 species of plants. In the gardens stands Latrobe's Cottage, the modest home of Victoria's first governors. The oldest building in Melbourne is on the grounds of another park, Fitzroy Gardens. This is the birthplace of Captain James Cook, which was brought from England and reconstructed here, right next to the Parliament.

The construction of Parliament House began in this early period of the city's history. Australia's federal government met there from 1901 until 1927, when it moved to Canberra. Another imposing example of Victorian architecture is the nearby Royal Exhibition Building. It was here that the parliament first came together to establish the country's constitution. This building, notable for its 60-metre high dome, was built in 1880 by David Mitchell, father of the world-renowned singer Nellie Melba.

Small business and big business meet on the corner of Collins and Swanston Streets. On Collins Street are found those business enterprises requiring the most fashionable address, as well as luxury hotels and the city's most expensive stores. Nearby is St. Paul's Cathedral, also begun in 1880. Opposite stands a cathedral of commerce, Flinders

Street Station, with its highly ornamented facade in the French Renaissance style.

Flinders Street Station lies directly on the Yarra River. On the opposite side of the river stands the Victorian Arts Centre, with its tall steel tower. The Arts Centre was Melbourne's answer to the Sydney Opera House. Both the city and state made sure that it would make a big splash. The theatre complex has three stages, one of which can accommodate an audience of two thousand. The concert hall can seat 2,500 people, and the art gallery boasts numerous works of art, both from Australia and abroad. In front of the museum, one can see works of art of another kind — the distinctive yellow and green trams that constantly roll by. Though only a few of these are still in operation, they remain an emblem of the city's historic past.

Even though the trams offer a very pleasant ride, in the inner city the tourist will hardly find them necessary. Almost all the sights are within comfortable walking distance — among these are the museums on Latrobe and Little Lonsdale Streets. The technologically inclined will certainly want to visit the Science Museum, although its location is a bit out of the way. One of the most popular attractions here is the *Polly Woodside*, a fully restored sailing ship.

Most visitors to Melbourne will want to make a trip into the surrounding countryside, though the idea of 'surrounding areas' has to be understood in the rather spacious, Australian sense. Included then on the itinerary will be Ballarat, some 120 km to the northwest, and Phillip Island, about 130 km to the southeast. This island, named after the first governor of the prison colony, is famous not only for its koala bears, but also its penguin parade. Every evening, promptly at sunset, some hundred little penguins set off from the waters where they spend their days, to the caves in which they pass their nights. With park rangers standing by, tourists flock to watch the penguins' comical progress. Leaving the relative safety of the water, the tiny penguins gather together in small bands, as they are too frightened to strike out for shelter on their own. If, while crossing the sand, one in the group loses heart, all of his compatriots will join him in a mad rush back to the sea, only to reassemble and try again a few minutes later.

Adelaide

Adelaide has been called the 'Athens of the Southern Hemisphere' and the 'Edinburgh of Australia' because of its vibrant cultural life. The capital of the state of South Australia has led the way in this respect for the rest of the continent. In 1974, the year that saw the opening of the Sydney Opera House, Adelaide established the Festival Theatre, a striking architectural achievement. With its completion, countless cultural organisations, including a symphony orchestra, theatrical and ballet companies, and galleries, finally found a home. The Festival Theatre offers suitably spacious conditions, and has room for three theatres, of which the largest can seat almost two thousand spectators (there is also room for an open-air theatre in summer). Every two years, the internationally recognised Adelaide Festival of Arts takes place. It is always held in March, in a park on the banks of the Torrens River. During the festival Adelaide becomes the cultural centre of Australia and is besieged with visitors, who come to enjoy the concerts and performances by artists from all over the world.

In addition to the Festival Theatre with its continuing cultural programs, three other

In the heat of the summer Bermuda shorts are acceptable dress for businessmen.

theatres and the State Opera Company beckon to the visitor. Five art collections, as well as numerous private galleries, compete for the attention of the million or so residents of Adelaide. The government of South Australia has invested a great deal of money in cultural affairs; the Festival Theatre alone cost (at the time) 20 million Australian dollars. The multi-faceted manifestations that art assumes have always been encouraged in Adelaide even if, at times, they were not high on the list of priorities of other regions in Australia.

According to its citizens, Adelaide has a long tradition of interest in art and culture. They boast that they live in the only major city in the country that was not founded by convicts. Free settlers established themselves here, about ten kilometres above the mouth of the Torrens, soon after their arrival in

South Australia. Their first point of debarkation, in 1836, was Kangaroo Island. Two years later they moved up-river because of the abundant supply of fresh water. Among the English settlers was the land surveyor, William Light, who, for that time, was a visionary in his plans for the city to come. He conceived of an urban environment where the river would divide the residential and commercial sections of the city, and ringing the city would be a girdle of greenery. (This green belt still exists and is one of the most valued aspects of Adelaide today.) All of this would be connected by especially broad avenues, which even today can bear the load of the automobile traffic of its one million inhabitants. One hardly notices that the centre of Adelaide is one of the most active commercial areas in Australia, even as businessmen in pinstripe suits, carrying cases, hurry past the skyscrapers lining King William Street. The most upscale addresses are not, however, on King William Street. They are to be found on North Terrace, overlooking Torrens' riverside park. Here stand buildings designed in the Victorian or classical style: the Art Gallery of South Australia, begun in 1895, which houses the largest collection of aboriginal art and artifacts in the world; Government House; Adelaide University, whose oldest building dates from 1882; Parliament House; the Holy Trinity Church of England, built in 1838; the old train station, which has been turned into a casino; and Ayers House, the stately residence of Henry Ayers, who was elected premier of South Australia seven times, and who gave Ayers Rock its name.

Adelaide's nearness to the river and abundant parklands can make the visitor easily forget that it lies quite close to the ocean. But Adelaiders certainly remember this, especially around Christmas time when the summer sun burns in the heavens — then, they pack up their bathing suits and hit the beach at Glenelg, or a little farther on to Kangaroo Island, where the attractions include rich and diverse flora and fauna, and the wild and beautiful south coast. The island is about 145 kilometres long and, at its widest point, 55 kilometres across. One-fifth of the island is devoted to national parks or nature preserves. Only two roads cross this, the third-largest island in Australia. Its unspoiled character has been, for the most part, maintained. Worth seeing are, not only the kangaroos, but the sea-lions of Seal Bay, who are so unimpressed by humans that the visitor can walk freely among them.

Another reason to visit the island is a remarkable area inland: Barossa Valley, a lovely region settled primarily by Germans.

This lodge at the foot of the MacDonnell Ranges in central Australia offers accommodations to travellers.

The valley runs for about 30 kilometres and is known for its wine, which the German emigrants brought from their homeland. The first vines were planted in 1847. Today the valley boasts over thirty of the best-known and most commercially successful vineyards in Australia.

Alice Springs

It takes two and a half hours to fly from Adelaide to Alice Springs, a small town in the middle of the continent that, for Australians, embodies the myth of the outback. At one time or another, almost every inhabitant of the well-populated south and southeast coasts plans a trip to this red, bone-dry region of Australia, though not that many actually get there. Its name has been immor-

talised in Neville Shute's novel *A Town Like Alice*, which is set in the outback and conveys a vivid sense of life in this remote area. For the first two hours of the trip the passenger can see only barren landscape, occasionally marked by a dry river bed, and then in the distance the first signs of the town can be made out at the base of the MacDonnell Mountains.

In 1871, an expedition that was laying telegraph wire for the first time across the continent, discovered a spring of fresh water, a find more valuable than gold. Soon Alice Springs, because of its location right in the middle of the country, had sprung up as a telegraph post, and a way station for those travelling in the interior. Even today, visitors can sense some of the early pioneer spirit, although Alice Springs now benefits from all the trappings of civilisation. The town's main

A telegraph station in Alice Springs, a town built in the heart of the outback.

sources of revenue are the cattle ranches that surround it and, more significantly, tourists, who use it as the jumping-off spot for tours of Ayers Rock. But there are interesting things to see within the town itself — the Flynn Memorial Church, for example, dedicated to the memory of the Reverend John Flynn, who founded the 'Royal Flying Doctor Service'. Early in the century, Flynn gathered together an intrepid corps of flyers to bring medical assistance to the sick-in-need, in the isolated areas of the interior. Today the 'Flying Doctors' have become a nation-wide organisation. Doctors stay in touch with their patients by radio, and now by computer; there has even been a popular television series based on their exploits. Also broadcast on radio is 'School of the Air', which provides education to the children of widely scattered farmers in the outback. Both stations are open to visitors. Another source of revenue are the camel ranches that can be found outside the town. Ambitious ranchers brought the camels in from Arabia; there are also large herds of wild camels that were originally brought from Afghanistan, which were used as pack animals during the construction of the trans-continental railroad, but now roam free.

Ayers Rock

Since an airport was built at Ayers Rock, many tourists prefer to fly there directly, rather than to travel the 473 km by road from Alice Springs, to see what is undoubtedly Australia's premier attraction. This sandstone outcropping rises 348 metres above the plain and has a circumference measuring almost nine kilometres. For over 600 million years, wind and water have left their imprint on the rock, and from close-up, the seemingly smooth rock face is seen to be as porous and wrinkled as an elephant's skin. But nonetheless there are smooth passages, which can prove tricky for climbers trying to scale its round back. Every year, a number of climbers meet with injuries, and sometimes, even fatal accidents.

Ayers Rock was named after a South Australian politician and, like many dramatic natural formations, is considered sacred by aborigines. In the 1980s the rock, which they call Uluru, was handed over to the local aboriginal population by the government. An agreement was reached whereby a few holy places at its foot were declared off-limits to tourists. The whole of Ayers Rock is now a national park, and the aborigines share the task of overseeing it. On the outskirts of the park, a brand new resort has sprung up; Ayers Rock Resort is distinguished by an elegant architectural design that blends in with its desert surroundings. Most visitors stay at least one night to experience the remarkable play of sunlight on the mountain, at sunrise and sunset.

Also belonging to the Uluru National Park are the Olgas, which lie at a distance of about thirty-five kilometres from Ayers Rock. These huge domes rise dramatically from the flat plain, as if hurled onto the ground by the hand of some giant. At 450 metres high, Mount Olga is the highest formation in the chain. Winding through the eroded rocks are precipitous ravines, which are home to some rare species of plants. Visually, the Olgas are even more imposing than their better-known neighbour, Ayers Rock.

A stately home in Western Australian is built in America's ante-bellum style.

Perth

The new airport in Ayers Rock Resort allows the visitor to approach Ayers Rock directly from the east coast, and from there you can catch a direct flight to Perth, which is on the west coast. It is very likely that the sun will be shining when you land there, because no major city in Australia has more hours of sunshine — eight a day, on average — than Perth. The climate in Perth is extremely pleasant, and in July, the coldest month, the temperature averages about 13 degrees Celsius, while in the heat of the summer the thermometer stays around 28 degrees and, if it gets too hot, the natives know that the afternoon will bring the Fremantle Doctor, a cooling breeze that is named for its healing properties. It blows from the sea and first touches Fremantle, the harbour-town, before

moving on to Perth. It is not surprising then, that Perth, the capital city of Western Australia, has such a relaxed atmosphere. Even the skyscrapers, corporate residences of mining, insurance and banking, that line the lagoon, look like holiday resorts. The lagoon, fed by the Swan River, was the main attraction for the first settlers, who were won over by this delightful location.

On May 2, 1829, Captain Charles Fremantle arrived at the mouth of the Swan River, and claimed the entire coastal region of New Holland, as Western Australia was then called, in the name of His Royal Britannic Majesty. But it took decades for Perth to come into its own. When gold was found in the interior at Kalgoorlie and Coolgardie in 1890, Perth became a wealthy city almost overnight. Some handsome buildings dating from that epoch still stand today. Most, how-

ever, were replaced in the 1970s when, during a new mineral boom, dollars rushed in and real-estate developments sprang up, with little attention paid to historical considerations. That explains the stark contrast between the lovely, old Victorian style buildings, and modern glass and concrete towers.

The Western Australia (W.A.) Museum, which is situated in a Georgian house built in 1856, describes this process in detail. Visitors should take the time to wander around the city on foot, to uncover the remnants of Perth's historic past. This is not so challenging an undertaking since the city is quite compact. The Western Australia Government Travel Centre on Hay Street, the main shopping street, provides a brochure listing historic walks. One of the oldest buildings still standing is the Old Courthouse that dates from 1836; many of the official buildings were erected a bit later, in the 1850s, when cheap labour was still to be had from the convict population. Examples from this era are the Deanery, City Hall on Hay Street, the newly renovated Majestic Theatre, the Treasury Building, the Old Perth Boys' School, the Cloisters, the Postal and Telephone Museum, and Government House. The governor's residence was erected between 1859-1864 and was modelled after the Tower of London. It has the air of a fairy-book castle, and its architectural style, as noted in a recent guidebook, "expresses the nostalgia the early settlers felt for their homeland".

Three art collections in Perth are worth a visit: The Western Australian Gallery, which offers a good overview of contemporary Australian and Pacific Art, the Aboriginal Traditional Art Gallery, and the previously mentioned W.A. Museum, which also holds a large collection of aboriginal art. A notable attraction of this museum is its meteorite collection. The largest meteor on display weighs over eleven tonnes.

Perth is as well known for its parks as for its museums. Especially delightful is Kings Park, which lies on the outskirts of the city. Most of the park has been preserved as unspoiled wilderness.

Fremantle

If you have some extra time to spend in this area, Fremantle, 19 kilometres from Perth, is well-worth seeing. This small town at the mouth of the Swan River was founded at the same time as Perth and has preserved some of the architecture of that period. This gives the town a nostalgic quality, and it also does honour to the town's fathers, who had the foresight to begin the work of preservation. From Perth you can reach Fremantle by bus or train, but the most scenic way to go is by boat. Travelling downstream you pass the Royal Perth Yacht Club, which, in 1983, laid claim to the most prestigious prize in the sailing world, the Americas Cup. After 132 years of unsuccessful attempts, this was the first time that a foreign rival managed to wrest the cup from the American team. The winning ship was the *Australia II*. The Australian team could now defend the cup on their own coasts, and that led to the development of new marinas in Fremantle, and hotels and casinos in Perth. The cup returned to America in 1987.

The competition for the cup is but one chapter in the unfolding saga of seafaring in Australia. This story is made clear by a visit to the Western Australian Maritime Museum. A visit to the Fremantle Museum will illustrate how intimately the history of the town is bound up with maritime history.

An old mining structure in Kalgoorlie, centre of Australia's gold country.

One of the earliest stone buildings in Fremantle was the prison, which was first used in 1831 and, because of its twelve-sided construction, was called the Round House. Today there is a Prison Museum, but it is not located at the Round House. It lies at the site of another prison that was built in 1851 and was in use until 1991. Another attractive sight is the Fremantle Markets, with its Victorian facade. It was built in typical Australian style, with a roof providing shade.

The isolated nature of Fremantle and Perth in the vast desert waste of Western Australia, means that most tours have to travel long distances. The most popular bus trips are, east to Wave Rock (near Hyden), or north to the Pinnacles. Both are a full day's journey, there and back. Wave Rock is a fifteen-metre high rock outcropping that looks like a frozen wave and through a long chem-ical process has taken on a striped pattern of different colours. Geologists suspect that this rock has been standing for hundreds of millions of years. North of Perth is Nambung National Park. There a sandy desert surrounds the Pinnacles, another geological rarity. Like stalagmites or tombstones, they rise up to six metres high in the flat desert land, like needles sticking out of the sand. Geologists believe that many of them are double or triple this height, but have been covered up by the sand. How these stone fingers came to be, nobody really knows.

Kalgoorlie/Coolgardie

Made from human hands are Australia's famous gold fields, about an hour's flight

The beach of Heron Island in the Great Barrier Reef.

Hannan's town blossomed. Current witnesses to this prosperous era are fine buildings such as the Post Office, Town Hall and the Exchange Hotel. Nearby is the Museum of the Goldfields, which has a collection of aboriginal artifacts as well as plenty of information on the history of the region. Next door to the museum is the British Arms pub, which has the distinction of being the narrowest bar in Australia. Here is where the Golden Mile begins, although Mount Charlotte is the only one of the mines that is still in operation. The other mines are picturesque relics, much favoured by photographers. There is one mine farther on that has been open since 1968, and it is known as the Hainault Tourist Mine. As the name indicates, its main business is catering to visitors, who can travel sixty metres down through the tunnels. First dug out at the turn of the century, the mine today offers a glimpse into the working methods of professional miners.

Those who would like to try their hand at prospecting can easily find what they need in Kalgoorlie. Everything from gold pans to electronic metal detectors can be rented in the town's general stores.

Darwin

The story of Darwin, the capital of the Northern Territory, is also closely connected to the search for gold. The natural harbour was discovered by J.C. Wickham in 1839. Wickham was the captain of the *HMS Beagle*, on which Charles Darwin sailed. So in memory of the scientist, Wickham named the bay Port Darwin. The new port, however, seemed destined to go the way of all the other short-lived settlements on the tropical north coast. The discovery of gold at Pine

from Perth. Kalgoorlie is the centre of this region. The first place that gold was discovered in this dry, forbidding outback area was Coolgardie. Today practically a ghost town, it survives on tourism and memories of its better days. In 1892, a miner found a lump of gold in this region weighing 15.7 kilograms. Soon 15,000 people had flocked into the wilderness (little wonder that word got out quickly!), even though there was no supply of fresh water. In its heyday, the town could boast two commodity exchanges, three daily newspapers and six banks, all housed in stately mansions. But the town soon ran out of luck. The gold was mined out, and those who chose to stay lived on little more than a few nuggets and the hope of a big strike. Coolgardie's handsome town hall and its no less impressive railway station stand as reminders of the town's former glory. Today,

they are both museums devoted to one theme: gold.

Kalgoorlie still lives off this glittering metal, although not exclusively. The residents have, for some time now, realised another kind of gold mine: tourism. Tourists are especially important because of continual fluctuations in the world-market price of gold. The Mount Charlotte Mine still produces gold today. It sits in the middle of the Golden Mile, a strip of land that at one time contained the richest gold mines in the world. The founder of the mining operation was an Irish prospector named Paddy Hannan. He set out from Coolgardie and discovered gold 40 kilometres away, in what is now the centre of Kalgoorlie. A bronze statue of Hannan stands at an intersection in town, where he freely dispenses the only commodity as precious as gold here: water.

Creek after a few years improved the situation, but there were still obstacles to overcome. The extreme heat and humidity threatened to wear down the inhabitants; even more destructive have been the frequent cyclones. During the Christmas season of 1974, Cyclone Tracey practically devastated the city. At times there has been talk of abandoning the city altogether, especially in the wake of the destruction caused by Japanese bombs during World War II. Darwin was the only city in Australia that lay within the range of the Japanese, since they had already established a foothold in Papua New Guinea. Many historic buildings were the victims of the bombing campaign, and Tracey levelled almost all of the rest. Despite these setbacks, the citizens decided to rebuild their city, but this time strived to make it cyclone-proof. Faced with this challenge, it is not surprising that aesthetic considerations were not a high priority. The new casino, however, manages to be both securely built and architecturally pleasing. For the rest, an abundance of tropical plants ornament the dreariness of the typical construction of the mid-seventies. Accordingly, remnants of Darwin's architectural past are extremely rare, but despite all this misfortune, Government House, with its 70-metre high stone roof, has remained, standing through the storms of nature and war. This white, colonial-style building is also known as Seven Gables. Work was started on it in 1870 but took seven years to complete. It is still in use as the seat of government and for this reason is rarely open to sightseers.

Only a handful of other buildings from the nineteenth century are still standing. Among them is Brown's Mart, which has a curious history. Built in 1885, it has served as a police station and a brothel, among other things. Today, it houses a theatre. Even older

Darwin's Casino Hotel with its futuristic architecture.

is the Fannie Bay Gaol, a prison built in 1883 that is now under the aegis of the National Trust. One year younger is the Old Admiralty House, which has housed both the police and courts of law. The most frequently visited of these old buildings is, without a doubt, the Hotel Victoria (on Smith Street, the main shopping thoroughfare). Built in 1890 its Victorian style pub, nicknamed Vic, is still a popular meeting-place, especially for young people. The many beer cans emptied here have been carefully welded together to create a fantasy ship. This sea-worthy craft features prominently every June during the 'beer can regatta'. Those who love the ocean have to confine themselves to this kind of entertainment during sea-wasp season. The poisonous sting of these jellyfish can be fatal. You can observe these, and other, dangerous denizens of the sea, as well as beautiful varieties of tropical fish, at little peril at the Indo-Pacific Marine Aquarium.

For those who are interested in more conventional sights, the Botanic Gardens, opened in 1891, are well worth a visit. Set in a large park, they were almost entirely destroyed by Tracey, but thanks to the tropical climate most of the species have recovered. If you would rather see these tropical plants in the wild and meet up with crocodiles outside of the reptile farms on the outskirts of the city, you can go on a safari or wilderness tour. Darwin is the starting point for tours into Kakadu National Park, one of the largest parks in Australia. It is located a good two hundred kilometres to the east of Darwin, but a well-paved road makes the trip an easy one. Kakadu National Park not only features abundant wildlife; it also contains fine examples of aboriginal rock art. Accom-

An embassy in Canberra shows a distinct Chinese influence.

modations can be had in the town of Cooinda or at the Gagudju Crocodile Hotel, which from the air is seen to have the shape of a crocodile. This is, indeed, Crocodile Dundee country.

Cairns

There is a direct flight from Darwin to Cairns, the state of Queensland's northernmost city and the centre of the fastest growing region in Australia. Where once only hibiscus bloomed, now tourism booms. Rumours abound about ambitious development plans. The pace of change here is swift indeed.

The greatest appeal of Cairns is its proximity to the Great Barrier Reef, the largest living coral reef in the world. It also lies close to the rainforest in the interior, which UNESCO declared a world heritage site at the end of the 1980s. This put the government on notice that the forest had to be protected.

Cairns is an ideal spot for sport fishermen. From September to December, when the mighty black marlins are running, the marinas in front of the town are crowded with lavish yachts. Almost all of these yachts belong to overseas visitors. During this time there are sure to be more millionaires in Cairns than in any other spot in Australia. But even in the off-season, the town benefits from a steady stream of tourists.

Certain attractions have been refurbished to take advantage of the tourist trade. An historic railroad winds its way over 34 kilometres and through 15 tunnels, to Kuranda on the Atherton Tablelands. Some of the trains make stops at scenic overlooks for photography. There are also regular tours to Daintree National Park and Cape Tribulation. The National Park, containing one of the last great rainforests in Australia, was the centre of a heated dispute between developers and conservationists. Cairns is also the departure point for safaris into the outback.

But as mentioned above, the principal attraction is, without a doubt, the Great Barrier Reef. The quickest way out to the reef is by plane or helicopter. Some firms offer seaplanes that land right by the reef. Many of the islands can be reached on a day-trip by ship. The reef is actually composed of two types of islands. Some islands are the peaks of underwater mountains, while others are made of coral that has been revealed by a decline in the sea level, or hurled upwards by geologic events. On a fast boat you can get to these two different kinds of islands that make up the reef, in just one day. The real reef islands are actually only the surface of the expanse of coral.

The Great Barrier Reef

This most famous coral reef in the world is 2,000 kilometres long, and about 20 to 50 kilometres away from the mainland. It stretches over a surface of about 200,000 square kilometres and is some 15,000 years old. The approximately 700 islands and sandbanks — most of them uninhabited — that it comprises have, for the most part, been incorporated into a national park. Unfortunately, the tiny coral, the builders of this masterwork are now under threat. Starfish prey on them in increasing numbers. As the coral die, the food supply on which the abundant marine life thrives, vanishes.

An even more serious threat comes from man himself, with his carelessness having already endangered the fragile ecology of the reef. Tourists, despite strict regulations against disturbing the reef, inadvertently, if not, deliberately, cause much damage. Business enterprises in search of oil, natural gas and minerals have contributed to the destruction of vast sections of the reef. In the face of these threats, the Green Party in Australia and other like-minded groups are redoubling their efforts to protect this unique underwater treasure.

These environmental organisations have called for a halt to tourist developments on the reef. The two-dozen or so islands that do have hotels on them, appeal to a widely varied clientele. The northernmost, Lizard Island, is frequented by sport fishermen and divers. Green and Fitzroy Islands are close in to Cairns, and cater to day-trippers from the mainland. The most expensive is the tropical Dunk Island. Farther south is Bedarra — a small, exclusive retreat. Among the rare resort islands in Australia are Hinchinbrook, which is somewhat larger than most of the other islands on the reef, and the upscale island Orpheus, which is also home to the marine biology laboratories of James Cook University. Magnetic Island lies directly in front of the coastal hamlet, Townsville, and a part of its residents live full-time on the island.

Farther south, the sensational Whitsunday Archipelago begins. Hamilton, and the neighbouring islands of Daydream, South Molle, Lindeman and Brampton are family-oriented. Long Island, on the other hand, attracts a young, sporty crowd. The two southernmost islands, Great Keppel and Heron, lie on a line with the town of Rockhampton. Great Keppel Island has always been a romantic getaway spot, and it pro-

motes itself to a younger audience. Heron Island lies about 70 kilometres off the coast. Nearby is Green Island, the only real coral island of this group.

These paradisiacal islands are naturally perfect for water sports. The same holds true for most towns on the adjacent mainland, which are transit points for the island but have, in the process, become tourist attractions themselves. This is the case, as we have seen for Cairns, Townsville and Rockhampton, but even more so, for Port Douglas and Mission Beach. All these places offer everything you might need for snorkelling and diving, and there are many diving schools that will teach the beginner how to enter the enchanted underwater world of the reef in style.

Brisbane

The capital city of Queensland lies on a bend in the Brisbane River. Once a sub-tropical retirement community, it has grown to become the third largest city on the continent. Brisbane City Hall is a good example of the tempestuous development of recent years. The 91-metre high tower, replicating the style of the Italian Renaissance that once dominated the city, has almost been obscured from view by the numerous surrounding sky-scrapers. Brisbane underwent a real estate boom in the 1980s, though some of the most ambitious projects had to be abandoned when financing fell through.

There have been some horrible architectural mistakes. A prime example is the highway that runs along the river. Now tour boats dock in the shadow of concrete posts when they return from the ocean, or Moreton Bay, or the upstream koala reserve at Lone Pine Sanctuary.

Lone Pine Sanctuary, eleven kilometres from the center of Brisbane, is one of the institutions that works to prevent the extinction of these marvellous animals. Part of their work is to establish breeding programmes, and also to study and combat the diseases that have decimated the koala population. About one hundred koalas live in Lone Pine. Other inhabitants of the preserve include kangaroos and wallabies.

On the south bank of the river lies the Queensland Cultural Centre, an attractive complex that includes a theatre, art museum and concert hall. There is also a fine park adjacent to it. The park is open 24 hours a day, and park rangers guard the lagoon, the man-made rainforest and world environmental display, which describes the earth's different climatic zones. On the opposite side of the river, the city is filled with uninspiring office buildings, built right up against various historical sites. Among the latter are the Presbyterian Church, whose image is reflected in the glass of a facing skyscraper, and the Old Government Building, out of place in its concrete surroundings.

In the midst of the building boom, many historical building were torn down almost overnight. Fortunately, the tip of the half-island on which the city is situated was spared from the mania for development, because the Botanic Gardens was located here (a new Botanical Garden has since been established on the outskirts of the city, on the slopes of Mount Coot-tha). The lookout point here provides the best view of the city and the Brisbane River, as it winds down to Moreton Bay. It was in 1823 that John Oxley landed at the river's mouth and set out upstream to explore the river. The news of his discovery led to the establishment of a penal colony here some years later. From this epoch dates the historic windmill, which was turned by convict labour on calm days. The convicts have vanished, but the windmill still stands, as a favourite vacationing spot for their descendants.

National Parks

Australia has more than 2,000 national parks, nature preserves and wildlife sanctuaries, in every climatic zone from tropical rainforest to the desert of the interior. Almost all of these parks have information stands and camping areas. Some, but not all, offer hotel or motel accommodations. Here are some that will amply repay the time it takes to visit them.

The coastline in the Northern Territory abounds in dramatic bays and inlets.

KU-RING-GAI CHASE
SYDNEY, NSW

This park lies on a strip of land that extends into Sydney Harbour. It contains more than 100 hundred kilometres of coastline and is rich in animal life. Between May and July, the lucky visitor can observe the mating rituals of the lyrebird. Aboriginal rock art can also be seen here. The park lies about 25 kilometres north of Sydney.

KOSCIUSKO
COOMA, NSW

The park, 6,900 square kilometres in size, lies in the Snowy Mountains, which include Mount Kosciusko (at 2,228 metres it is the highest mountain in Australia). In the winter it offers fine skiing; in spring and summer trails are bedecked with colourful wildflowers. It is located about 500 kilometres to the southwest of Sydney.

FRANKLIN AND GORDON WILD RIVERS
STRAHAN, TAS

This wide-ranging and still-undisturbed river system runs through the wilderness about 200 kilometres west of the capital of Tasmania, Hobart. It was the object of a bitter national debate. One part of the river was destined to be used to generate hydroelectric power. But for the first time environmentalists were able to prevail in their fight against industry, and the river remains unspoiled.

PORT CAMPBELL
WARNAMBOOL, VIC

Situated about 250 kilometres southwest of Melbourne, Port Campbell can boast what many consider to be the most spectacular stretch of coastline on the continent. Here are picturesque rock formations, the best-known being the Twelve Apostles. The park runs parallel to the panoramic Great Ocean Road, which hugs the coastline.

FLINDERS CHASE
KINGSCOTE, SA

This park lies on the western tip of Kangaroo Island, the third largest island off the coast of Australia. Much of it is covered by eucalyptus trees, the natural home of koalas. From time to time the careful observer can catch a glimpse of them, although they are naturally shy of humans. Kangaroos and emus are more frequent visitors to the picnic areas. In another park on the island, sea-lions abound and they are quite unafraid of humans.

thirteen ravines with towering walls. It is a place of rare, natural beauty. The park is about 30 kilometres northeast of Katherine, from where you can take a bus tour through the ravines. But you have to be careful of crocodiles here; they can be deadly.

MORETON ISLAND
BRISBANE, QLD

The island of Moreton, only 20 kilometres east of Brisbane, the capital of Queensland, is famous for its strikingly high sand dunes. The 285-metre Mount Tempest is the highest sand mountain in the world. Almost 90% of the island, on which there are no paved roads, belongs to the national park.

Each state has its own national park service, and a department of conservation and environmental protection. The central office for the Australian National Parks and Wildlife Service is located in a suburb of the nation's capital, Canberra.

The Outback

It is difficult to define the boundaries of the outback with any degree of certitude. It is the wild land in the heart of the red continent — part sand desert, part bush and part stony mountain ridges. Every state (except for Tasmania and Victoria), has a region in the outback that is still home to some aboriginal tribal groups. Unlike some of their people who have been victimised by white civilisation, these groups still maintain a vital connection to the culture and myths of their ancestors.

Aborigines leading their traditional nomadic existence are infrequently met with. However, some of them who live on reserva-

NAMBUNG
CERVANTES, WA

This is another coastal park; much of it is covered by sand dunes. It also goes by the name of its best-known feature, the Pinnacles. These rock formations are remarkably varied in size and shape, and loom over a barren landscape. Numerous theories have been proposed regarding their origin. To get to Nambung one must travel north from Perth, for about 250 kilometres.

KAKADU
JABIRU, NT

This expansive park in the 'Top End', the damp tropical north of the Northern Territory, is one of the few places on earth that, on account of its cultural significance as well as its natural beauty, has been placed on the reg-

ister of world heritage sites. Examples of aboriginal rock art that are thousands of years old, and open country that is flooded annually are the main attractions. Hundreds of varieties of animals dwell here — from giant crocodiles to brightly coloured cockatoos. The best time to visit is during the dry season between July and September, when animals can be observed gathering at the water holes. Some industries, such as uranium mining, have been granted special permission to exploit the natural resources of the park. But their work is carefully monitored to minimise injury to the environment.

KATHERINE GORGE
KATHERINE, NT

The aboriginal name for this park is Nitmiluk. The Katherine River empties into

tions in the outback do go on pilgrimages to their holy places to immerse themselves in the world of the Dreamtime.

The visitor needs special permission from the state government to travel to most of the aboriginal settlements. But in most states aborigines will accompany tourists into the outback and show them the secrets of tracking game, survival in the wilderness and the tribal way of life. The various state tourist bureaus can provide further information.

To tour the outback on one's own requires careful preparation. The favorite route across the continent is the Stuart highway that runs from Adelaide to Darwin. This main road is paved, but if you want to venture off of it into the wilderness, you will need a four-wheel drive vehicle. Those who choose to take this route should carry extra gas, food and plenty of water. If you experience car trouble or meet with an accident, you might have to wait for some time before help arrives. The general rule is to always stay near your car. Never walk off alone because solitary strolls through the outback can have deadly consequences. If you are planning to travel in remote areas, you should inform the police or park rangers.

There are almost no settlements in the outback, only widely scattered stations where farmers offer food and simple accommodations. Two towns have, however, developed a viable tourist industry: Coober Pedy in South Australia and Longreach on the border of Queensland. Coober Pedy thrives from opal mining. Here, hundreds of miners search for these profitable semi-precious stones. To escape the oppressive heat, some of the residents of this peculiar town have moved into caves, which they have comfortably furnished. Since the completion of the Stuart Highway, Coober Pedy has become a popular destination for tourists. It is also easy to get

Whether in the high plains of Queensland...

to Longreach. This little town has played a role in the history of Australian aviation, and it was here that Qantas Airways built its first airplane hangar. Nowadays, sightseers can visit the Stockmen's Hall of Fame and the Outback Heritage Centre, with collections devoted to the exploration of the outback and ways of survival in this desolate region.

Australians call their cowboys 'stockmen', even though today they travel in helicopters rather than on horseback. Many stockmen are aborigines. With their knowledge and experience of the outback, they are best qualified for the job.

The Bush

The Australians distinguish between the outback and the bush. While the outback is a

wide expanse of barren land fit for little except cattle ranching, the bush lies nearer to the coast and is better for agriculture. In the hot, damp north, cattle ranches predominate; in the cooler south, sheep herding is the primary activity. The bush has left an indelible mark on Australians' sense of identity. Although the outback retains a kind of mythological significance for them, the bush is the setting of much Australian folklore. Popular writers such as Banjo Paterson and Henry Lawson have drawn upon it to articulate many of the unique characteristics of Australian life.

Going bush is, for many Australians, even beach lovers, a favourite way to spend a vacation. These open areas, lightly wooded with eucalyptus, are ideal for camping, hiking and horseback riding. The mountain ranges that line the coast beckon to visitors as well

...or the wetlands of Kakadu National Park: Everywhere there are glimpses of nature's beauty.

(especially those visitors who have extra time to spend and have already seen the more noteworthy sites). Once you get to know the country a bit, and have had the chance to sample the simple hospitality of the Aussies who live outside of the big cities, you will find a stay in the bush (whether in a small hotel or a guest-room in a farmhouse), to be a most memorable experience. Sheep ranches can be a lot of fun to visit. There are about 140 million sheep in Australia, and many of the ranches provide accommodations for visitors. A short stay can be a delightful way to get away from it all, though it may leave you with a false, idyllic impression of the sheep ranchers' way of life which, in reality, can be quite a hard one.

Many farms offer guests the opportunity to ride on horseback or make jeeps available for expeditions into the countryside. If you're lucky to be there on the weekend you may be invited for a picnic or go to a country horse race, where the betting is taken very seriously. Evening is the time for gathering around the 'barbie' (the barbecue, that is), for thick steaks and ice-cold bush beer. Then off for the obligatory visit to the local pub (which can be thirty or forty kilometres away) where the natives will regale their visitors with stories of bloodthirsty dingoes, flying emus, and kangaroos carrying koalas in their pouches. It's best to take some of what you hear with a pinch of salt.

You can find places to stay in the bush in every state in Australia. State tourist offices provide more detailed information. Many little towns and farms attract visitors with the opportunity to try one's hand at prospecting for precious stones or gold. Others offer special trips for fishermen, led by guides who know the best fishing holes and streams. What is more, a vacation in the bush is normally inexpensive and lets more adventurous visitors experience first-hand, the warmth and hospitality of typical Australians.

The Islands

Australia is itself an island continent. But surrounding it are many smaller islands — some like Kangaroo Island in the south, lying just off the coast; others like Lord Howe or Norfolk Island lie out in the ocean, at a distance of many hours' flying time. Many of these islands live off the tourist trade, even those that do not have the fame of the Great Barrier Reef as a draw.

Even in Tasmania, the largest island in Australia, and a state in itself, tourism is an important part of the economy, eclipsed only by forestry and agriculture. Off the coast of Tasmania lie small, little-known islets such as Flinders and King Islands, which are dedicated to nature preserves, vacation cottages and outdoor sports.

Vacation and sporting facilities can be found on almost any island. Rottnest Island in Western Australia is situated not far from the town of Fremantle. Its main attraction are the quokkas, small pouched animals that can only be found here. When the first Europeans arrived they thought the quokkas were a kind of rat, hence the name 'Rat Nest Island'. Today both tourists and quokkas enjoy themselves — the former taking photos of the appealing little creatures, the latter fattening themselves off the generosity of their visitors.

The animals on the large tropical islands off the coast of Darwin are less cuddly. These twin islands have beautiful beaches but swimming is best left to the sharks that circle

A beach on Kangaroo Island, which lies off the south coast of Australia.

the area in search of prey, and the poisonous, potentially lethal, jellyfish. This is also the home of the Tiwi tribe, whose culture has diverged in many ways from that of the aboriginal population on the mainland. To learn about their culture and customs it is best to travel with a tour guide. Today, the tribe is part owner of these islands.

North of Brisbane, though still forming a part of the chain that makes up the Great Barrier Reef, is Fraser Island, the largest sand island in the world. One-third of its land is now a national park. Part of the land is thickly wooded, but four-wheel-drive vehicles can penetrate the unspoiled countryside to reach the dunes, or one of two hundred small lakes. This is an especially good place to catch sight of the often shy dingo, Australia's wild dog.

Lord Howe Island lies about 600 kilometres northeast of Sydney, a tiny dot in the vast Pacific Ocean. Two mountain peaks rise from the forest and that, combined with a turquoise blue lagoon, make it a photographer's paradise. Lodgings, while comfortable, are not luxurious. Nonetheless, it can be quite an expensive place to visit, because of the cost of the flight. It has a narrow landing strip that can only accommodate small planes carrying a limited number of passengers.

More than twice as far away lies Norfolk Island, 1,450 kilometres from the Australian coast. This volcanic island is only eight kilometres long and four kilometres wide. The worst offenders of the prison population were confined here, and ruins recall this epoch of the island's history. In 1856, the 194 inhabitants of Pitcairn Island settled here

after famine forced them to leave their home. The Pitcairn Islanders descended from the mutineers of the *Bounty*. Many of them eventually returned to Pitcairn, but some stayed on Norfolk. In addition to its history, its tax-free shopping attracts a good many visitors to the island today — an example of how Norfolk has successfully exploited its status as a self-governing territory. In addition, it has its own customs service and issues its own stamps.

Sydney Gears Up for the 2000 Olympic Games

On the 15th of September this year, all eyes will be on Sydney, Australia, as the 'Harbour City' plays host to what has undoubtedly become the most important sporting event in modern times — the Olympic Games.

Since September, 1993, when it was awarded the right to host the Games of the XXVII Olympiad, Sydney has been preparing for what is expected to be the most spectacular celebration of sport and culture ever witnessed. This being the first Games of the new millennium, huge efforts are being made to ensure that the event is extra special, and one which Australia, and indeed, the rest of the world, will continue to remember for decades to come.

This will be the first Olympic games ever to be held in Sydney, and accordingly has generated great excitement among Sydneysiders. Games organisers have been in the grips of preparing for an unprecedented number of visitors from every corner of the globe. Much is being done to ensure that the entire city remains safe, clean and secure, that transportation to and from the Olympic venues runs efficiently, and that the needs of

Sydney SuperDome — View from Olympic Plaza at twilight

every competitor and spectator are catered to.

The Sydney Organising Committee for the Olympic Games (SOCOG) was established on November 12th, 1993, and since then it has been working closely with the International Olympic Committee (IOC) in Lausanne, Switzerland, the Australian Olympic Committee (AOC), and the Olympic Co-ordination Authority (OCA), to make sure that the 2000 Summer Games are nothing short of successful. From the construction of Stadium Australia, the Aquatic Centre and the Velodrome, to marketing, ticketing, security, and the organisation of both the Opening and Closing ceremonies, no effort has been spared to make this year's Games the best the world has ever seen.

Sporting Facilities and the Olympic Village

Most of the facilities for the 2000 Olympics have already been completed. These facilities, located in various areas all around Sydney, will be used for different events and have mainly been constructed using state-of-the-art materials and technology.

Perhaps the most impressive is the Olympic Stadium (also called Stadium Australia), which is situated at Sydney Olympic Park in Homebush Bay (on the banks of the Parramatta River). Costing approximately $690 million (Australlian), construction started in September, 1996, and took about two and a half years to complete. Fourteen storeys high (at its highest point), and consisting of eight levels, the Olympic Stadium

is the largest outdoor venue in modern Olympic history. It will seat an estimated 110, 000 people during the Games. The Olympic Opening and Closing ceremonies, track and field events, and the finals (gold-medal) game for soccer, will all be held in the Stadium; during the Paralympics, the venue will be used for the Opening and Closing ceremonies, and athletics.

The 400-metre athletics track laid over the Olympic Stadium is made from vulcanised rubber and is said to be about five to ten percent softer than the one used at the 1996 Games in Atlanta. Additional features of the Stadium include a 105-metre by 68-metre grass football field, an electronic scoreboard, and a video screen.

Other events, such as boxing and basketball, will be held at the Entertainment Cen-

Stadium Australia — Aerial view of stadium . View from the south west

tre and Exhibition Halls in Darling Harbour (in the heart of the city), while equestrian events will be held at the Equestrian Centre in Horsley Park. The Velodrome in Bankstown will be home to indoor cycling competitions, and if beach volleyball is your cup of tea, then make your way to ultra-hip Bondi Beach, east of Sydney.

Approximately 15,400 Olympic competitors and officials are expected to reside in the Athletes' Village from September 2nd to October 4th, and from October 11th to November 1st, the Village will accommodate around 7,500 Paralympic competitors and officials. Also called Olympic Village, the site has an area of about 100 hectares, and is situated in Newington, near Olympic Park and

about 15 kilometres from the centre of Sydney. Construction of the Village started in July 1997, and is scheduled for completion about three months before the start of the Games. The Village, to be powered mainly by solar energy, will offer a wealth of facilities including shops and other commercial services, and leisure and recreational activities. Containing 1,150 permanent dwellings and specially-designed modular homes, the Village will be a safe and secure environment for all its residents. Buses will ferry athletes from the Village to their specified venues of training and competition.

When the Olympic and Paralympic Games are over, Athletes' Village will undergo further construction to become a

prestigious new suburb for Sydney. It is expected to house around 5,000 people and will have lots to offer, including a primary school and other handy amenities.

What Visitors Can Expect

Visitors to the Games will be suitably impressed with all the Olympic City has to offer. For starters, one can expect highly efficient transportation between the main metropolitan areas and Olympic venues. The Olympic Roads and Transport Authority (ORTA), set up by the New South Wales Government in 1997, has been given the major task of ensuring that transport services operate efficiently during the Games, and that the city's roads are not only safe, but also sophisticated enough to cope with greater-than-usual volumes of traffic. ORTA has been working closely with the Department of Transport, the Roads and Traffic Authority (RTA), the State Rail Authority (SRA), Bus 2000, the State Transit Authority (STA), the Taxi Council, as well as the New South Wales Police and local communities, in order to achieve its goals.

ORTA is responsible for the transport of spectators during the course of both the Olympic and Paralympic Games, and many believe that this will be the biggest public transport operation the country has ever seen. Although an estimated 3,350 buses will operate during the Games (about 1,700 will be reserved for spectators), trains are expected to be the main form of transport for spectators. The brand-new railway station at Olympic Park will hook up to the city's main Western railway line, and railway stations along the designated routes will be upgraded. Most of these stations will also improve the services and facilities available to people with disabilities or mobility difficulties, so be on the lookout for lifts or ramps, continuous hand rails, and hearing aids at ticket windows.

Australians were given top priority when tickets to the Games went on sale in 1999. Approximately 75 percent of all tickets were made available for sale to Australians, with the rest going to overseas visitors, and local and international media representatives. Tickets to prime events, such as swimming, and the Opening and Closing Ceremonies, were snapped up almost immediately, leaving many would-be spectators disappointed. It is, however, good to know that there are some events for which tickets are not required, and these include road cycling, race-walking, sailing, the marathon and the triathlon. These events allow free viewing, and tens of thousands of spectators are expected to turn up.

For visitors wanting to buy a little piece of Olympic history, there is always The Olympic Store. Stocking a plethora of collectables, including jewellery, pins, plush toys, posters, stationery, medallions, clothing, magnets, keyrings, bedding, and even tableware, The Olympic Store has branches all over Sydney (including the Arrivals Hall at Sydney International Airport), and in David Jones Department Stores across the country.

Unless hotel reservations have already been made, finding a place to stay during the Games might prove somewhat difficult for visitors (especially since half of Sydney's 40,000 hotel rooms have already been reserved by SOCOG). An official Residential Accommodation Program has been set up, offering visitors a range of private, furnished accommodations for the duration of the Games. This service operates through a database system that matches available rental properties with visitors' budgets and requirements. For many, finding accommodation in areas well away from the city centre has also been a good option, although this will mean longer travelling times to and from Olympic venues.

During the Games, security will be tight: venues have been fitted with expensive, high-tech equipment, and will be monitored closely to ensure the safety of all. Extra security measures will also be taken at Sydney Airport.

Celebrating the Olympic Spirit

The Summer Games will officially begin on Friday, the 15th of September, and end on Sunday, the 1st of October, with more than 10,000 athletes from 200 countries expected to participate in 28 different sporting events. The athletes, to be joined by about 5, 000 Olympic officials, will arrive from nations as far away as Botswana and Angola in Africa, Bhutan and Mongolia in Asia, Guatemala and Uruguay in Central America, and Iceland and the Ukraine in Europe.

The Games this year are a tribute to the athletes of the world, and nothing is more symbolic of this than the Sydney 2000 Olympic logo. The 'Millennium Athelete', so-called because it depicts the figure of an athlete, is a pastiche of shapes and colours that best represent the beautiful Australian landscape, and its original inhabitants, the aborigines. The legs of the athlete, for example, are symbolised by a boomerang, coloured red to represent Australia's desert interior, while the 'smoke' from the Olympic Torch takes on the outline of the sail-like roof of the Opera House, and is coloured blue to represent water.

The Olympic Torch will begin its journey around Australia on the June 8, 2000 — a hundred days before the start of the Games. Said to be the longest Torch Relay in Olympic history, the torch will be carried by 11,000 Torchbearers, and travel a distance of about 27,000 kilometres—across the remote outback on a chartered airline, through the Nullabor Plain on an Indian Pacific Train, and on a surf boat at Bondi Beach. Described as modern and innovative, the Olympic Torch has an environmentally-friendly inner combustion system, and an unusual design inspired by the Sydney Opera House, the blue Pacific Ocean, and the gentle curve of the boomerang. Michael Knight, President of SOCOG and Minister for the Olympics, believes the Torch to be a strong representation of the key values of the Games, and at its unveiling in March 1999, remarked that it reflected "the egalitarian spirit of Sydney and Australia, the commitment of the athlete and Olympism, and the inspiration of innovation."

The Opening Ceremony, to be held at Olympic Park, is set to be a colourful and dazzling affair. Australian Ric Birch, Director of Production for the 1984 Los Angeles Olympic Ceremonies, and Executive Producer of the 1992 Barcelona Olympic Ceremonies, will act as Director of Ceremonies for the Games in Sydney this year. Although little has been said about what to expect for this first event of the Summer Olympics, Birch has hinted that Australia's unique multicultural society will feature as an important theme.